建築家の設計プロセスを徹底解剖していく，大好評のPLOTシリーズ

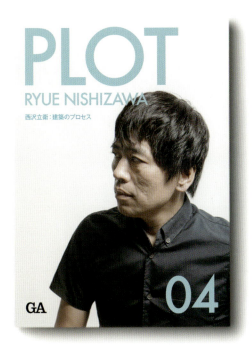

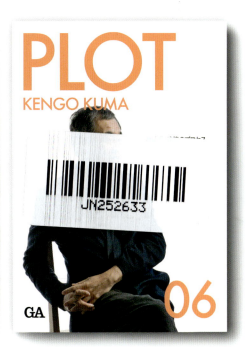

西沢立衛：建築のプロセス

収録作品
十和田市現代美術館，豊島美術館，
軽井沢千住博美術館，小豆島の葺田パヴィリオン

インタヴュー
西沢立衛の現在形 [聞き手：二川由夫]
軽井沢千住博美術館について [聞き手：二川幸夫]

size: 257×182mm, Japanese text only, 216 total pages　¥2,300+tax

伊東豊雄：建築のプロセス

収録作品
多摩美術大学図書館，座・高円寺，
台湾大学社会科学部棟

インタヴュー
伊東豊雄の現在形 [聞き手：二川由夫]

size: 257×182mm, Japanese text only, 272 total pages　¥2,500+tax

隈研吾：建築のプロセス

収録作品
下関市川棚温泉交流センター，
アオーレ長岡，浅草文化観光センター

インタヴュー
隈研吾の現在形 [聞き手：二川由夫]

size: 257×182mm, Japanese text only, 272 total pages　¥2,500+tax

PLOT 07
妹島和世：建築のプロセス

新刊

収録予定作品
豊田市生涯学習センター逢妻交流館
京都の集合住宅
日立駅自由通路及び橋上駅舎
なかまちテラス 小平市立仲町公民館・仲町図書館

2015年6月25日刊行予定

井上章一 現代の建築家

日本の現代建築を、ふりかえる。
今、建築家たちはどこにむかおうとしているのかを、考える。
そんな文章を、古い建築にもこだわりつつ、
これから書きついでいくつもりである。

私たちには、モダニズムの前後、第二次世界大戦の前後で断絶しがちだった、建築の見方があります。そんな中、長野宇平治、伊東忠太からはじまり、坂倉準三、丹下健三、菊竹清訓は勿論、磯崎新、安藤忠雄に至る、明治から新しい国家をつくりあげてきたキラ星のような建築家たちを一緒くたにし、ひとつながりの視点でつづられた井上流のものがたりは、これまでの建築界内の通説や、一般化したイメージを覆す、かつてない目からウロコの建築家論になりました。明治に生まれ、モダニズムの波を越えて、現代に至る日本の建築家たち。日本の自我は、どのように建築や都市にあらわされてきたか。建築家のあゆみを、社会のありようから考える、画期的な日本近代化論としても読める一冊です。

（「ささやかな前口上」より）

A 5 版上製本／総五〇四頁／三三〇〇円+税

新刊

安西水丸 地球の細道

一九九九年から二〇一四年の十五年間にわたり
安西水丸が綴った、旅のエッセイとイラスト集

二〇一四年三月に急逝された、イラストレーターで作家の安西水丸さん。この訃報を受け、『GA JAPAN』誌上で十五年間（一九九九年三六号〜二〇一四年一二七号）にわたって、水丸さんに連載いただきました「地球の細道」全九一話を一冊にまとめました。「地球の細道」では、水丸さんが日本だけでなく世界各地を訪ね歩き、その土地にまつわる歴史や人物のエピソードを紹介するとともに、水丸さんご自身が感じたことを、気負いのない文章と独特のほのぼのとしたイラストで綴っています。特にお好きだったお城に加え、世界中の食や絶景、映画、絵画、音楽、天気の話等々、水丸さんならではの旅の楽しみ方を伝えてくれる一冊です。巻頭には、水丸さんが訪れた地をプロットした地図を付け、あとがきは、親交のあった建築家・妹島和世さんに寄せていただきました。水丸ファンは勿論のこと、どなたにも気軽に楽しんでいただける、水丸版〈世界のガイドブック〉です。

A 5 版上製本／総三八〇頁／三二〇〇円+税

GA JAPAN
Global Architecture

日本の新しい優れた現代建築のエッセンスを主に国内に向けて発信する，隔月刊の建築デザイン専門誌。
建築思想，技術思想を照射しつつ，建築のデザインに迫る本格的建築総合誌です。

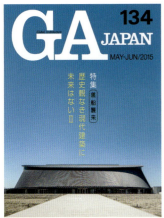

192 pages, 88 in color / Japanese text only
¥2,333

最新号
特集：歴史観なき現代建築に未来はないⅡ

黒船来襲に対する6人の識者の見解
日埜直彦，磯崎 新，石山友美，戸田 穣，藤森照信，デイヴィッド・スチュワート

作品
妹島和世　なかまちテラス 小平市立仲町公民館・仲町図書館
内藤 廣　静岡県草薙総合運動場体育館
柏木由人+Olivia Shih　同志社京田辺会堂
田邊 曜　旭町診療所
Herzog & de Meuron　ミュウミュウ 青山店
小嶋一浩+赤松佳珠子　流山市立おおたかの森小・中学校，こども図書館，センター
小嶋一浩+赤松佳珠子　立川第一小学校／柴崎図書館／学童保育所／学習館
飯田善彦　龍谷大学深草キャンパス 和顔館
日建設計　港区立小中一貫教育校 白金の丘学園

PLOT
隈 研吾「（仮称）飯山ぷらざ」編 phase 4：現場での決定事項

連載
二川幸夫の眼 7「石山修武」
地球の景色 3　藤本壮介
ロボットはコンピュータの夢をかたちにするか？ 7　竹中司＋岡部文／アンズスタジオ

GA広場
直島パヴィリオン／藤本壮介，小豆島のバス停／島田 陽，
The University DINING／工藤和美・堀場 弘・佐藤 淳・吉村 明，
The One 南園パヴィリオン／隈 研吾

Our subscription is available worldwide.

年間購読のご案内　どこよりも早く確実にお手元にお届けいたします

GA JAPAN

GA DOCUMENT

GA HOUSES

Contact us: **sales@ga-tbc.co.jp** (Overseas) / **order@ga-tbc.co.jp**（日本国内）

Please visit our website: **http://www.ga-ada.co.jp**

詳細はウェブサイトをご覧下さい。

GA HOUSES
Key to Abbreviations

ALC	alcove
ARCD	arcade/covered passageway
ART	art room
ATL	atelier
ATR	atrium
ATT	attic
AV	audio-visual room
BAL	balcony
BAR	bar
BK	breakfast room
BR	bedroom
BRG	bridge/catwalk
BTH	bathroom
BVD	belvedere/lookout
CAR	carport/car shelter
CH	children's room
CEL	cellar
CL	closet/walk-in closet
CLK	cloak
CT	court
D	dining room
DEN	den
DK	deck
DN	stairs-down
DRK	darkroom
DRS	dressing room/wardrobe
DRW	drawing room
E	entry
ECT	entrance court
EH	entrance hall
EV	elevator
EXC	exercise room
F	family room
FPL	fireplace
FYR	foyer
GAL	gallery
GDN	garden
GRG	garage
GRN	greenhouse
GST	guest room/guest bedroom
GZBO	gazebo
H	hall
HK	house keeper
ING	inglenook
K	kitchen
L	living room
LBR	library
LBY	lobby
LDRY	laundry
LFT	loft
LGA	loggia
LGE	lounge
LWL	light well
MBR	master bedroom
MBTH	master bathroom
MECH	mechanical
MLTP	multipurpose room
MSIC	music room
MUD	mud room
OF	office
P	porch/portico
PAN	pantry/larder
PLY	playroom
POOL	swimming pool/pool/pond
PT	patio
RE	rear entry
RT	roof terrace
SHW	shower
SIT	sitting room
SHOP	shop
SKY	skylight
SL	slope/ramp
SLP	sleeping loft
SNA	sauna
STD	studio
STDY	study
ST	staircase/stair hall
STR	storage/storeroom
SUN	sunroom/sun parlor/solarium
SVE	service entry
SVYD	service yard
TAT	tatami room/tea ceremony room
TER	terrace
UP	stairs-up
UTL	utility room
VD	void/open
VRA	veranda
VSTB	vestibule
WC	water closet
WRK	workshop/work room

表記価格に消費税は含まれておりません。

A.D.A. EDITA Tokyo

142

Contents／目次

- 8   Sean Godsell: Green House
  ショーン・ゴッドセル：グリーン邸
- 20   Wiel Arets: A' House
  ヴィール・ァレッツ：A' ハウス
- 32   Yo Shimada: House in Toyonaka
  島田 陽：豊中の住居
- 44   Clinton Murray + Polly Harbison: Balmoral House
  クリントン・マレー＋ポリー・ハービソン：バルモラル・ハウス
- 56   David Welsh + Christine Major: The Garden Project
  デイヴィッド・ウェルシュ＋クリスティーン・メージャー：ガーデン・プロジェクト
- 66   Satoshi Matsuoka + Yuki Tamura: House on Backyard
  松岡 聡＋田村裕希：裏庭の家
- 76   Yuri Naruse + Jun Inokuma: Split House
  成瀬友梨＋猪熊 純：スプリットハウス
- 84   Milano Salone Report 2015
  ミラノサローネレポート2015
- 92   Andrés Casillas & Evolva Architects: Mexican Contemporary House
  アンドレス・カシージャス＆エヴォルヴァ・アーキテクツ：メキシカン・コンテンポラリー・ハウス
- 106   Yutaka Yoshida: House in Kaita
  吉田 豊：海田の家
- 118   Casey Brown: Pacific House
  ケーシー／ブラウン：パシフィック・ハウス
- 130   Casey Brown: Barrenjoey House
  ケーシー／ブラウン：バレンジョイ・ハウス
- 142   Makoto Takei + Chie Nabeshima / TNA: Between Natsumezaka
  武井 誠＋鍋島千恵/TNA：夏目坂の間

《世界の住宅》142
発行・編集人：二川由夫
編集スタッフ：斎藤日登美，仲村明代

2015年5月25日発行
エーディーエー・エディタ・トーキョー
東京都渋谷区千駄ヶ谷3-12-14
電話 (03)3403-1581(代)
ファックス (03)3497-0649
E-mail: info@ga-ada.co.jp
http://www.ga-ada.co.jp

ロゴタイプ・デザイン：細谷巖

印刷・製本：図書印刷株式会社

取次店：
トーハン，日販，大阪屋
栗田出版販売，西村書店，中央社
太洋社，鍬谷書店

禁無断転載
ISBN978-4-87140-090-9 C1352

GA HOUSES 142
Publisher/Editor in Chief: Yoshio Futagawa
Editors: Hitomi Saito, Akiyo Nakamura

Published in May 2015
©A.D.A. EDITA Tokyo Co., Ltd.
3-12-14 Sendagaya, Shibuya-ku, Tokyo,
151-0051 Japan
Tel. (03)3403-1581
Fax. (03)3497-0649
E-mail: info@ga-ada.co.jp
http://www.ga-ada.co.jp

Logotype Design: Gan Hosoya

Printed in Japan by
Tosho Printing Co., Ltd.

All rights reserved.
Copyright of Photographs:
©GA photographers
All drawings are provided by
architects except as noted.

Cover: House on Backyard
by Satoshi Matsuoka + Yuki Tamura
Photo by Katsumasa Tanaka
pp.4-5: Mexican Contemporary House
by Andrés Casillas & Evolva Architects
pp.6-7: Barrenjoey House by Casey Brown
Photos by Yoshio Futagawa
English translation:
Lisa Tani (pp.84-90), Satoko Hirata (p.32,
p.67, p.77, pp.112-113), Erica Sakai (p.147)
和訳：原田勝之 (pp.10-11)，坂本和子 (pp.30-
31, p.50, p.65, p.102, pp.124-125, p.141)

SEAN GODSELL
GREEN HOUSE
Melbourne, Victoria, Australia

Photos: Yoshio Futagawa

Street elevation (veranda of original cottage) 道路面（既存コテージのベランダ）

Alterations and additions to a small heritage listed timber cottage in inner suburban Melbourne. Planning and heritage requirements and construction costs fundamentally drove the outcome of this project. Our client came to us wanting a new house. For reasons only known and understood by the local authorities the existing cottage was deemed to be of some historical significance. We disagreed with that assessment but to no avail. It was a case of limp-wristed facadism by the authorities and heritage 'experts'. Instead of abandoning our client we agreed to start from scratch, keeping the front section of the cottage and re-working it and then building a discrete fully new section at the rear of the block. I saw the project in a different light and chose to re-visit some projects that had inspired me as a young architect—Kazuo Shinohara's *House in White* and *House in Hanayama No. 3* and Tadao Ando's *Row House in Sumiyoshi* or *Azuma House* as it is sometimes known. The *Row House in Sumiyoshi* is a work of genius and I have written elsewhere about that building describing it as 'a seminal work of the second half of the twentieth century'.

In simple terms the cottage interior is remodelled to have a cathedral ceiling with a pair of timber posts supporting the ridge beam and two light cannons directing light to the centre of the single space formed by the demolition of an existing wall. A small courtyard bound by concrete walls separates the cottage from the small addition, evok-

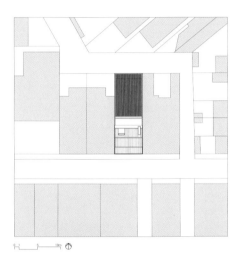

Site plan S=1:800

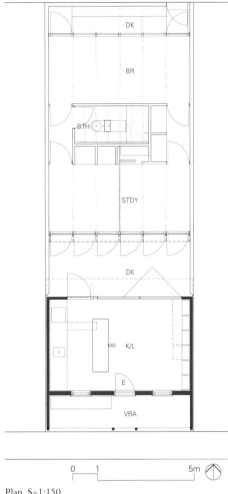

Plan S=1:150

ing the *Row House* in the process. To address issues of overshadowing and overlooking we kept the height of the addition low (3.0 meters overall) and to compensate for a lack of light we made the roof of the entire addition glass with an automated timber sunscreen. The sunscreen protects the occupant from summer sun but can be configured in a variety of ways to allow the ingress of winter sun. As the screen is operated from inside the appearance of the building changes. If the owner so desires they can use the roofscape as an additional outdoor living area.

We finished the design of this project at the same time that the RMIT design Hub was completed and it served as poignant reminder that the power of architecture is independent of scale.
Sean Godsell

Architects: Sean Godsell Architects—
Sean Godsell, principal-in-charge;
Hayley Franklin, project team
Clients: Peter and Janina Green
Consultants:
Perrett Simpson Stanton, structural;
Sean Godsell Architects, interior;
Filter ESD, environmental;
Michael Taylor Architecture + Heritage, heritage consultant; Plan Cost Australia, cost consultant; Meredith Withers, planning consultant
General Contractor:
Sargant Constructions Pty., Ltd.
Structural system: precast concrete and steel frame structure (rear), timber framed structure (existing cottage)
Major materials: steel, pre-cast concrete, glass, perforated aluminium, timber
Site area: 101.4 m²
Building area: 77.55 m²
Total floor area: 77.55 m²
Design: 2011-13
Construction: 2013-14

Veranda ベランダ

Post box 郵便受

メルボルン旧市街にある文化遺産として登録された木造のコテージの改修と増築の計画。文化遺産の計画規制と建設費用がこの計画の行く末を決定することになった。クライアントが必要としていたのは新しい住宅である。どうやらこの地域の自治体は様々な理由をつけて，この既存のコテージに何かしらの歴史的価値があると見なしていたようであった。私たちは異議を申し立てたが，認められることはなかった。これは行政官と文化遺産の「専門家」による怯懦なファサーディズムの一例である。そこでクライアントのために，全てを始めから検討することになった。コテージの正面は保存と改修を行い，背後には正面から完全に分離された新しい区画が建設されることになった。私はこの計画に異なる光をあてようと考えていた。そのためには若い頃，私にインスピレーションを与えてくれた幾つかの作品——篠原一男の「白の家」と「花山第三の家」，そして「東邸」としても知られる安藤忠雄の「住吉の長屋」——を再訪する必要があった。「住吉の長屋」は天賦の

View from north: sunscreen roof　北より見る：日除けスクリーンの屋根

才の作品であり，私はかつて，この建築のことを「20世紀後期の建築の出発点となる作品である」と書き記したことがある。

簡潔に言えば，このコテージは伽藍天井を加えて内部空間を改修し，一組の木柱が棟木を支えている。また，既存の壁を撤去して生まれた一体的な空間の中央に，直接光を引き込むことができるよう，二つの天窓が計画された。コンクリートの壁面で囲われた小さな中庭は，コテージと小さな増築部を切り離す役割を果たす。これは「長屋」を再現したものである。影が深いため，また，眺望を得るために，増築部の高さは（全体で３メートルと）低く抑えるように計画された。また，十分な光を得ることができないために，屋根全体は自動制御の木製の日除けの付いたガラスで製作された。日除けのためのスクリーンは居住者を夏の太陽から守り，冬の太陽を様々な方法で屋内へと引き入れることができる。スクリーンを内部から操作すると建築の見え方も変化する。オーナーが望むのであれば，ルーフスケープを屋外空間として利用することもできる。

この計画の設計はRMIT（ロイヤルメルボルン工科大学）のデザインハブの完成と同時期に完了したが，これは建築の持つ力が規模とは関係なく存在することを強く想起させてくれる。

（ショーン・ゴッドセル）

Sean Godsell / Green House　11

Sunscreen: close → open　日除けスクリーン：閉→開

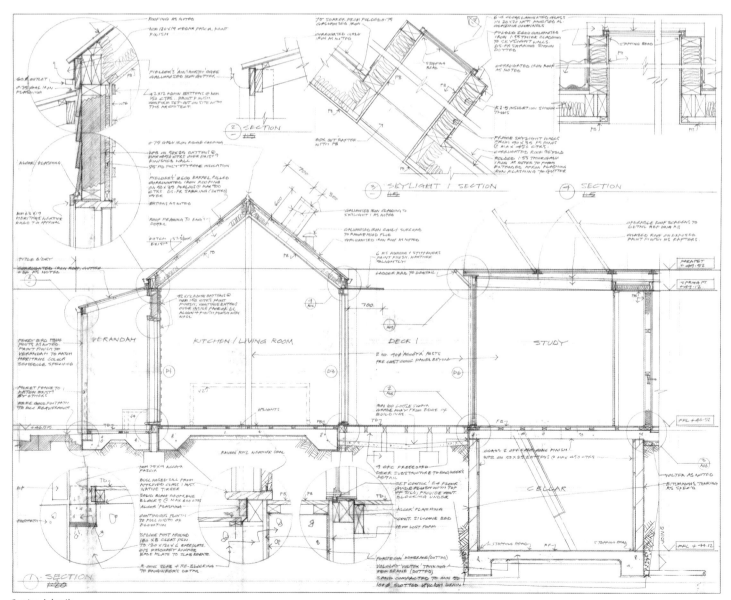

Sectional details

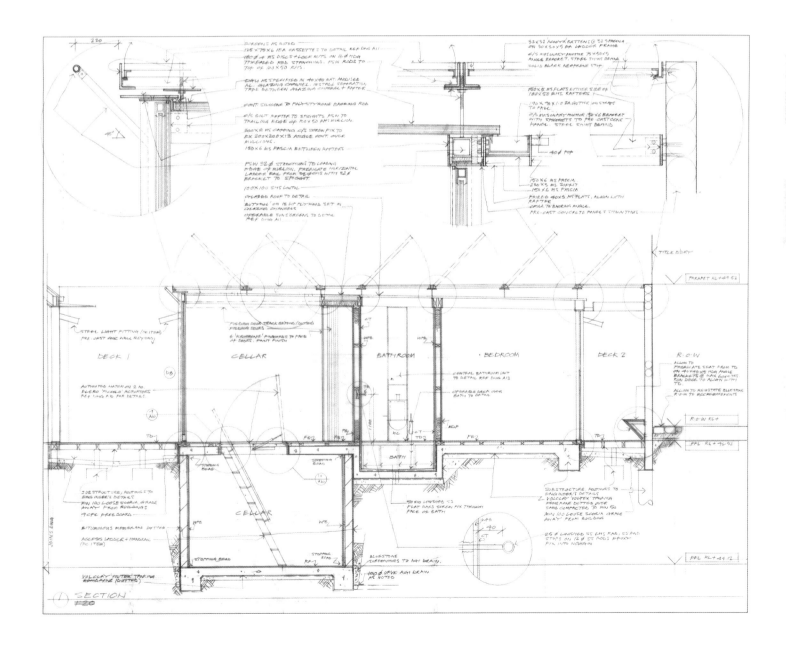

Sean Godsell / Green House

Kitchen/living room: looking west 台所／居間：西を見る

Kitchen/living room: looking east 台所／居間：東を見る

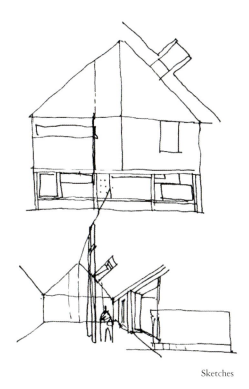

Sketches

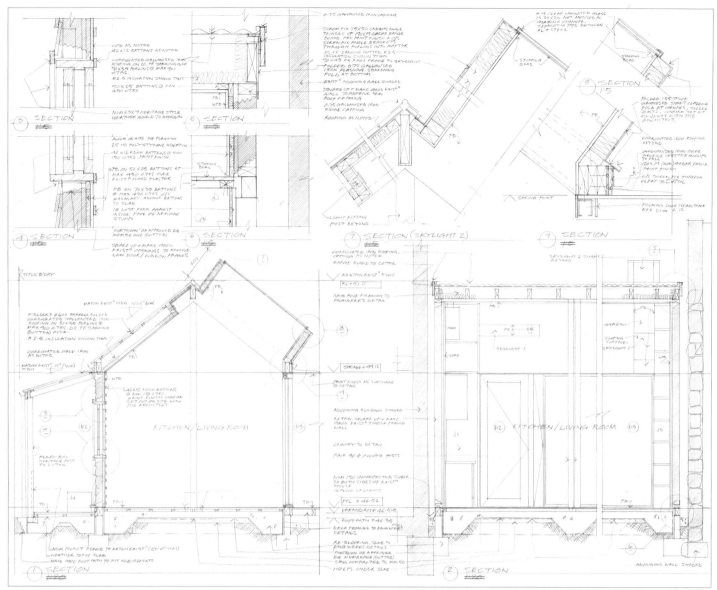

Sectional detail

Detail of glazed door ガラス戸詳細

Sketch

View from kitchen/dining room toward deck and study　台所／食堂より，デッキ／書斎を見る

View of study　書斎を見る

Bedroom　寝室

Detail of glazed ceiling and sunscreen
ガラス天井と日除けスクリーン詳細

View toward study from bedroom　寝室から書斎方向を見る

Bathroom　洗面室

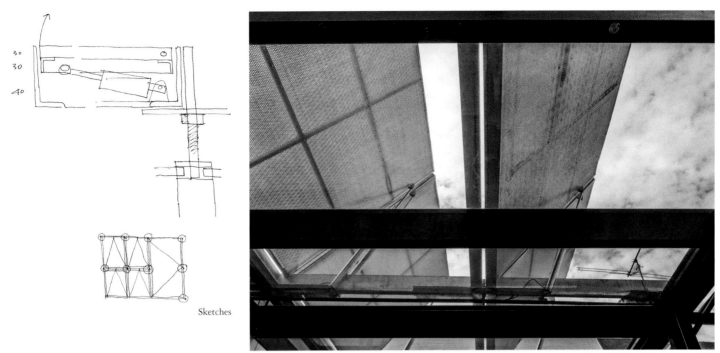

Sketches

Detail of glazed ceiling and sunscreen　ガラス天井と日除けスクリーン詳細

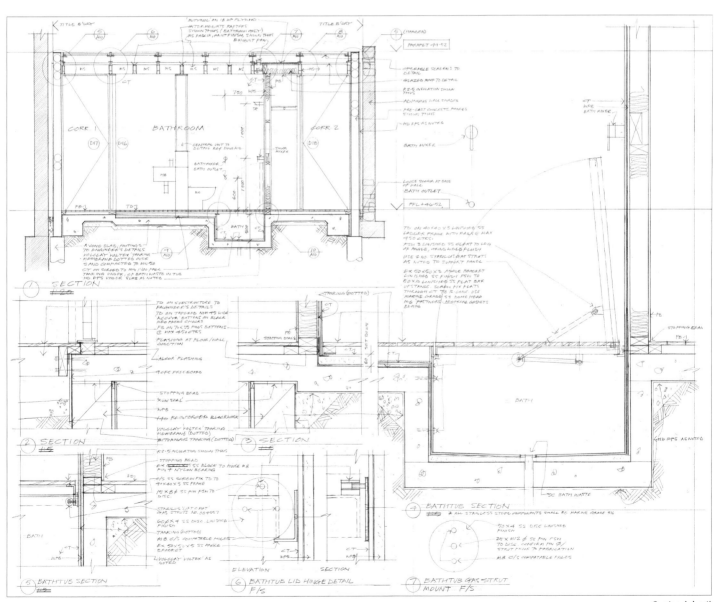

Sectional detail

Sean Godsell / Green House

WIEL ARETS
A' HOUSE
Tokyo, Japan
Photos: Yoshio Futagawa

Southwest elevation: dining room on right 南西面：右は食堂

◁ Overall view from south 南側全景

Aerial view of site

This compact private residence is nestled within the dense expanse of Tokyo—a neighborhood characterized by narrow streets and traditional low-rise houses—which borders a park heavily visited during the spring, when the city's cherry trees begin to bloom. Its 136 square-meter volume consists of four horizontally divided spaces, each connected by a minuscule sculptural spiraling staircase that, given the footprint of the house, allows for loft-like spaces within its intimate confines. Oversized windows punctuate the house, each with two layers of glazing; one is transparent and one is of the same relief glass that wraps the facade. These oversized windows, with their dual layers of glazing, can be countlessly reconfigured, to regulate the interior flow of daylight.

Both the transparent and relief glass of the house's windows slides on tracks, which extend to double the width of each, for unobstructed views. They extend to the floor, to ensure that the house remains responsive to passing street life. When closed, they cloak the house within an iridescent texture. On the first floor, one of these windows serves as the main entry, and slides open to reveal the kitchen. Each level has a different program: the lower two bedrooms, with a wooden ofuro, permeated by daylight via sliver windows that span the full length of the house at street level; the kitchen and dining room occupy the first floor; the living room the second; and the uppermost a master suite.

A small terrace is attached to the master bedroom, and it is expansive, relative to the house's size. Its northeastern wall is composed of the same textured glass that shields the house's glazing, except that there is no layer of transparent layer behind it, as the terrace is fully open to the exterior elements. When this glass wall is retracted, a view toward the park suddenly appears. When closed, the view is obstructed and the exterior space introverts, which allows for privacy within this publicly exposed level of the house. Conversely, southwestern wall of this terrace is also the pinnacle of the house's textured facade, into which a cut was created, which allows for ample amounts of interior daylight. The cut left a void in that facade, which created an enveloping terrace, open to the sky.

Subtly bold seen from afar, the house blends into its context. When all of its windows are opened, or when a combination of several windows are open and closed, the house morphs to expose its kaleidoscopic

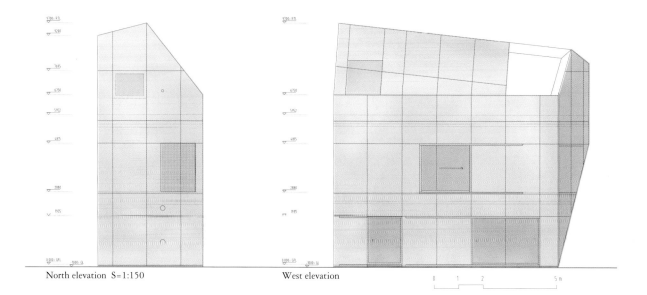

North elevation S=1:150

West elevation

Third floor

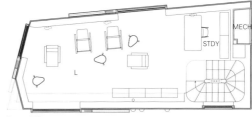
Second floor

First floor S=1:150

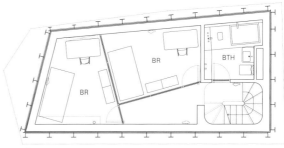
Basement

qualities to the immediate neighborhood and its residents. Structurally, the house is composed of concrete, and it is earthquake proof, in accordance with stringent local regulations. Due to the house's slender site, a fold was created along its southern facade, angled so that it retreats from the street at ground level, which provides just enough space for a *smart* car. Centrally sited within Tokyo, with the possibility to turn toward the city, or retreat into itself, in multiple configurations; A' House is an idiosyncratic private residence, engaged in a continual dialogue with its traditional Japanese context, while simultaneously anticipating the future.

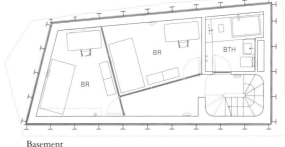

East elevation

South elevation

Entrance 玄関

Kitchen/dining room on first floor 1階，台所／食堂

Staircase 階段

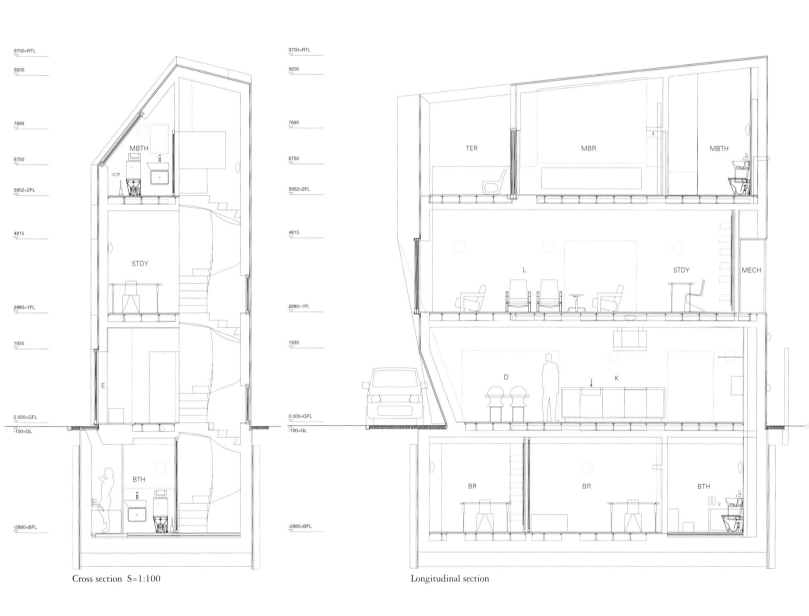

Cross section S=1:100

Longitudinal section

Wiel Arets / A' House

Living room on second floor 2階，居間

Downward view of study　書斎を見下ろす

View toward study from living room　居間より書斎を見る

View toward master bedroom from terrace on third floor 3階，テラスより主寝室を見る

Terrace テラス

△▽ Master bedroom on third floor 3階，主寝室

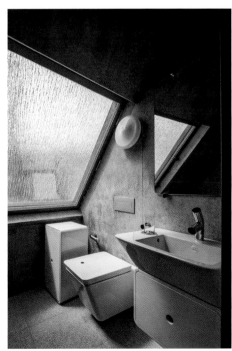

Master bathroom on third floor 3階，主洗面室

Architects: Wiel Arets Architects—
Wiel Arets, principal-in-charge;
Satoru Umehara, Alex Kunnen, project team
Collaborators:
Jörg Lüthke, Jean-Jacques Jungers,
Sadamu Shirafuji, Ilze Paklone
Local architects:
Tai Mikio Architect & Associates
Consultants:
LOW FAT structure Inc., structural;
EOSplus Co. Ltd., Comodo Co. Ltd., mechanical; Oskomera Group B.V., facade;
Saint Gobain Glass, manufacturer
General Contractor: Eiger Co. Ltd.
Structural system: poured in place concrete
Major materials: concrete, glass
Total floor area: 136 m^2
Design: 2007-09
Construction: 2009-14

Two bedrooms with skylight on basement: glazed partition　地下1階，天窓から光の差し込む二つの寝室：ガラスの間仕切り

Bathroom on basement　地下1階，浴室

　このコンパクトな個人住宅は，東京の密集した街並みが広がる一画に佇んでいる。狭い通りに昔ながらの低層住宅が建ち並び，街中の桜が咲き始める春には多くの人が訪れる公園に接している。延床面積136平米のヴォリュームは，上下四層に分割され，各階はごく小さい彫刻的な螺旋階段で繋がれており，この限られた占有面積において，居心地よいロフトのようなスペースが形成されている。透明ガラスと，外装と同じレリーフガラスによる2枚の大きな窓が建物にアクセントを与えている。この特大のガラス窓は，自然光を自在に室内へ取り込めるよう，開閉位置をそれぞれ自由に設定できる。

　透明ガラス，レリーフガラスどちらも，窓幅の倍の長さまで引き出すことができ，遮るもののない眺めを満喫できる。窓は床のレベルまで延ばし

View from northeast 北東より見る

て，通りを行き交う日常風景と呼応できるようにした。すべて閉じると，窓は，見る角度や光により様々な質感に変化する建物をくるむ外皮となる。1階の窓の一つがメインエントランスとなっており，引き開けるとキッチンが現れる。各階ごとに異なる機能が設けられている。地下1階には二つの寝室と木のお風呂があり，建物の全長にわたって道路レベルに設けられたシルバーの天窓から自然光が差し込む。1階にはキッチンとダイニングルーム，2階にはリビングルーム，3階には主寝室がある。

主寝室には小さなテラスが設けられており，この住宅の面積にしては開放感がある。北東面は窓に使われているのと同じガラスで覆われているが，透明ガラスの層はなく，テラスは外に全面的に開かれる。ガラス壁を引き込むと眺望が公園に向かって一気に開ける。ガラス壁を閉じると，眺望は遮られて内部化し，外に開かれたこの階でもプライバシーを確保できる。テラス反対側の南西面は，ユニークなテクスチャーを持つファサードの頂部に当たる場所で，一部を切り込むことで室内に十分な光を届ける。この切り込みによりファサードにヴォイドが生まれ，壁で囲い空に向かって開けたテラスがつくられた。

遠目にはいささか大胆な形だが，周辺環境に溶け込んでいる。窓が全部開いていたり，いくつかの窓が開いたり閉じたりすることで，この住宅は万華鏡のように変化し，近隣地域とそこに住む人々を映し出す。建物はコンクリート造で，地域の厳しい規則に準拠した耐震構造になっている。敷地が細長いため，南側のファサードを道路高さで通りから引き込む角度で折り込み，ちょうどコンパクト・カーのsmartが収まるスペースを設けた。東京の中心部に位置するこの住宅は，様々な状態に変化して街と向き合い，あるいは街の中に身を潜めることもできる。A'ハウスは日本の伝統的なコンテクストと常に呼応しつつも同時に未来を待ち望む，一風変わった個人住宅である。

YO SHIMADA
HOUSE IN TOYONAKA
Toyonaka, Osaka, Japan

Photos: Yoshio Futagawa

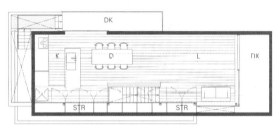
Second floor

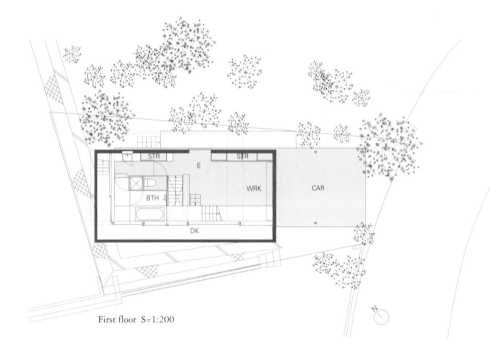
First floor S=1:200

Basement

Dynamic Abstractness
It might be my prejudice, but architectural space gradually becomes static, when impurities are reduced to be abstract. It also has an effect for various human activities and furniture to vividly come to front, but sometimes it appears they are being denied. My query was to find out whether it is possible to create space that has quality of, so to speak, dynamic abstractness, enabling space to all the more get settled when activities and things are mixed with the space and objects are flooded.

The site of the residence is narrow and long, irregular-shaped and sloped. The area is enforced with strict wall-setback restriction and also had shadow regulation. Under the limitations, we considered creating stretch of space by using mitigation of the regulation that permits decks and eaves to protrude over setback lines. Exempted from shadow regulation, the eaves height was decided to be less than 7 meters in two-story with one underground floor. The above-ground part is sliced into seven layers, shifted, stacked and eliminated to create deep pleated exterior look. The manipulation is similar to *House in Matsunoki (GA HOUSES 140)*, which was being designed at the same time. In *House in Matsunoki*, different materials were used to articulate segments, but in this residence, all are finished with white FRP, so that pleats can be made deeper both inside and outside. In this way, we tried to make relation with outer space, while protecting the inside with wrapping belt-like space. The shifted volume functions as a balcony, eaves and windows on the outside, level gaps are used for a desk, stair landing, alcove and shelves at inside. A nearby bush and a neighboring range of roofs are cut out horizontally by the window generated from the shifts. Stairs, benches and storages, made by connecting or blocking gaps and made like furniture, are mixed with things such as furniture brought by the residents. We hope it succeeded in gaining dynamic abstractness.
Yo Shimada

View from south　南より見る

Yo Shimada / House in Toyonaka

Overall view from east 東側全景

Architects: Tato Architects—
Yo Shimada, principal-in-charge;
Nobuhiko Sato, project team
Consultants:
Takashi Manda Structural Design—
Takashi Manda, Taijiro Kato, structural
General Contractor: Kohatsu co., Ltd.
Structural system: steel frame
Major materials: exposed concrete, glass, steel, plywood
Site area: 129.70 m²
Built area: 50.98 m²
Total floor area: 121.40 m²
Design: 2013
Construction: 2014-15

Longitudinal section S=1:200

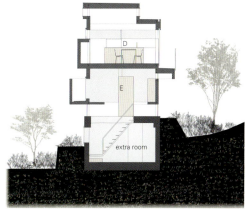

Cross section S=1:200

Yo Shimada / House in Toyonaka

Workspace: looking southwest from entrance 作業スペース：玄関より南西を見る

Looking northwest on first floor　1階，北西を見る

Workspace on first floor　1階，作業スペース

Looking southeast from bathroom: deck on right　浴室より南東を見る：右はデッキ

View toward storage from entrance　玄関より収納を見る

Looking southeast from deck on first floor　1階，デッキより南東を見る

Yo Shimada / House in Toyonaka　39

Staircase to second floor　2階へ通じる階段

Downward view from second floor: bathroom at end　2階より見下ろす：奥は浴室

View toward dining room/kitchen on second floor 2階, 食堂／台所を見る

〈動的な抽象性〉
ぼくの勝手な思い込みかもしれないのだけれど，建築空間から夾雑物を減らし，抽象的な空間にしていくと，だんだんと静的な空間になる。それは人間のさまざまな活動であったり，家具であったりが鮮やかに浮かび上がる効果もあるのだけれど，なにかそれらを否定しているように見えることもある。人々の活動や，事物が空間と交じり合って，物が溢れれば溢れるほど，かえって建築がまとまっていくような，動的な抽象性とでも言うべき質をたたえた空間をつくり出すことはできないだろうか。

この住宅の敷地は細長く，不整形でおまけに斜面になっていて，壁面後退の指定の厳しい地域で，日影規制もあった。そこでデッキや庇は壁面後退線にかからない法の緩和を利用して拡がりをつくり出せないかと考えた。日影規制を受けない軒高7メートル以下，地下1階地上2階建てとし，その地上部を7層にスライスしてずらしながら積層したり抜いたりすることにより襞深い外観をつくりだしている。その点では同時期に設計していた「松ノ木の住居」（『GA HOUSES 140』）と同じような操作だ。「松ノ木の住居」では分節をより強調させるために素材を切り替えたが，この住宅では，内外まで襞を深く展開するために全て白いFRPとしている。そうやって帯状の空間をまとわせて内部を守りながら外部との関係をつくることを考えた。ずらされたヴォリュームはバルコニーや庇，窓として機能し，内部ではその段差を机や踊り場，アルコーブ，棚とした。ズレによって生じた窓からは，隣地の草むらや，周辺の瓦屋根の連なりが水平に切り取られる。段差をつないだり，塞いだりするように家具のように誂えた階段やベンチ，収納が，住人の持ち込んだ家具などのモノたちと混じりあい，動的な抽象性を獲得できないかと考えた。

（島田 陽）

View toward living room over staircase on second floor　2階，階段越しに居間を見る

Looking northeast: kitchen (left) and dining room (right)　北東を見る：台所(左)と食堂(右)

CLINTON MURRAY + POLLY HARBISON
BALMORAL HOUSE
Balmoral Beach, Sydney, New South Wales, Australia

Photos: Yoshio Futagawa

View toward entrance from southwest 南西より玄関を見る

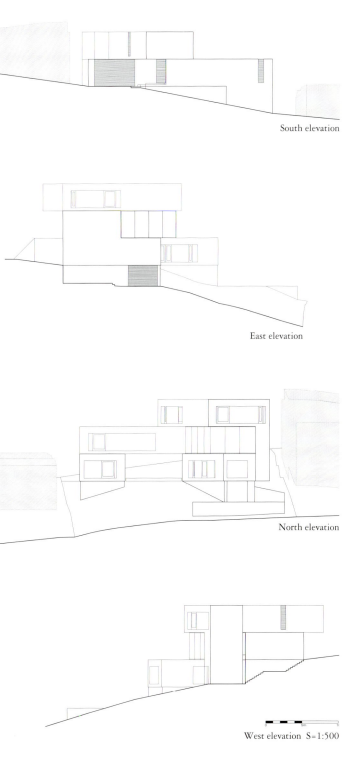

South elevation

East elevation

North elevation

West elevation S=1:500

Clinton Murray + Polly Harbison / Balmoral House

Entrance (left) and terrace (right) 玄関(左)とテラス(右)

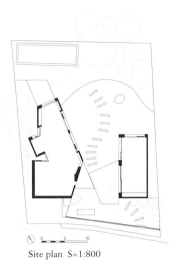
Site plan S=1:800

Architects:
Clinton Murray + Polly Harbison Architects in Association—Clinton Murray, Polly Harbison, principals-in-charge;
Nicholas Byrne, Vince Myson, project team
Consultants:
Ken Murtagh, structural;
Ralph Rembel, interior designer;
Daniel Baffsky, landscape;
Andre Tammes, lighting
General Contractor: Bellevarde
Structural system: off-form concrete
Major materials:
off-form concrete, blackbutt timber, brass
Site area: 1,172 m²
Building area: 450 m²
Total floor area: 450 m²
Design: 2012
Construction: 2013-14

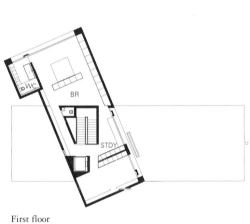
First floor

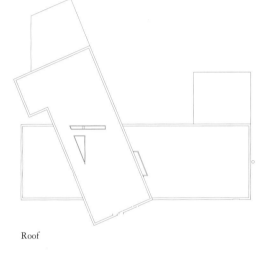
Roof

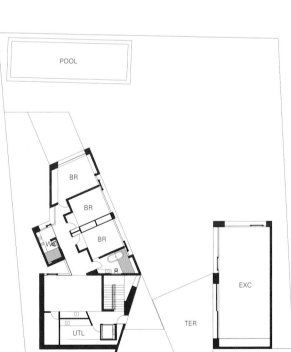
Lower ground floor

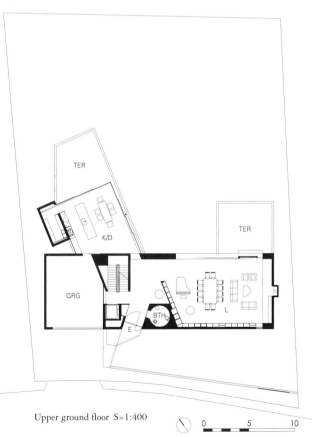
Upper ground floor S=1:400

Clinton Murray + Polly Harbison / Balmoral House

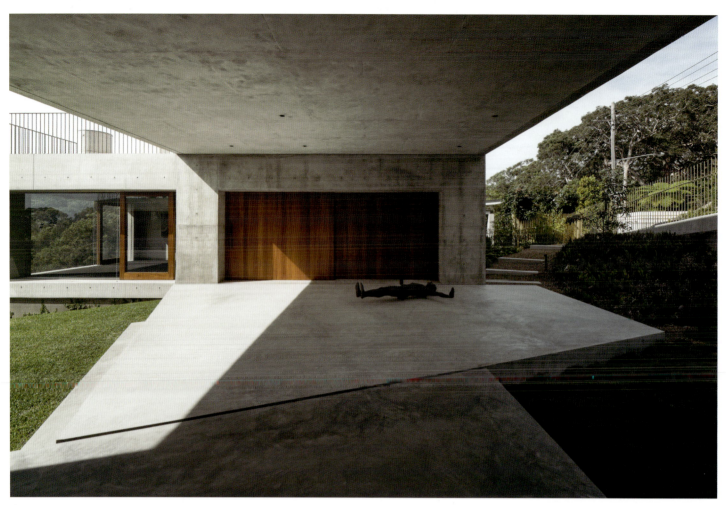
△▽ Terrace on lower ground level 地階，テラス

View from northeast 北東より見る

Our client's love of art inspired experimentation with sculptural forms that didn't compromise the functional brief of the house. First and foremost the house had to be a home, not an art gallery! Secondly our clients were determined we made the most of the beautiful views over the beach and to the harbour beyond. We looked to *Isamu Noguchi* for inspiration. His iconic sculptures curve and twist and link us to windows into other worlds.

The concrete sculptural form is a union between engineering and architecture, revealed as a series as boxes assembled to respond to views, sun and privacy requirements. Simple design principles of orientation, thermal mass and natural ventilation are fundamental to the design.

The critical moment in the design process was emphasising the opportunity we had to connect the house to the community. In an area typically dominated by high fences and street level intercoms, we've allowed passers-by to touch and feel the building and look through it to Balmoral beach. This experience is further enhanced by the careful positioning of selected artworks in the main under croft and garden beyond. One sculpture, a cast human form, lays passively, arms outstretched, feet pointing northward, waiting for commentary. A recent example from 2 small boys passing questioned the presence of a 'dead man' while the other responded, 'that's not a dead man, that's art!'

From within the house views are carefully edited and framed to create a sense of serenity and isolation within an urban context. To accentuate wall thickness, fixed glass windows are housed into the deep concrete reveals. All opening windows are framed in timber and slide on concealed tracks. Recessed in to the concrete above are operable retractable louvres. The whole house can close down against the dramas of Australian coastal living.

Housed within the building is a lifetime collection of sculpture and art. The individual needs and logistics of each artwork were considered like any other occupant. The stairwell is itself sculptural, carved from concrete and lit from above. The skylights create ever changing shafts of light that animate the experience of the sculptural objects placed within.

There is a consistent simple palette of timber and concrete, contrasting the rich tones and textures of the art collection. Interiors are a seamless extension of the architecture. An 'Yves Klein' blue ceiling floats provocatively above the main living room. The same disciplined design restraint is evident in the detailing of the building. External walls intentionally morph into internal walls. Soffits become ceilings, and when the 3.6m high doors all slide away, the kitchen becomes a part of the landscape, a nest in the trees, a safe haven.

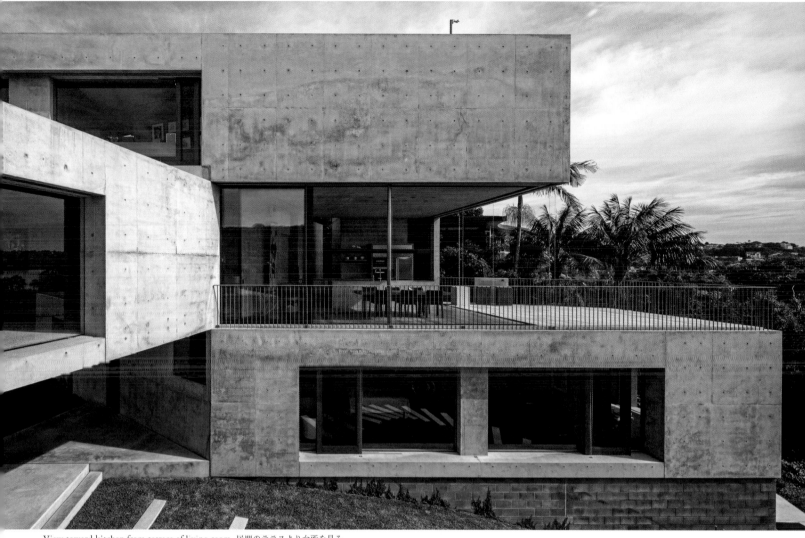

View toward kitchen from terrace of living room　居間のテラスより台所を見る

　私たちのクライアントは，芸術に触発された彫刻的なフォルムの試みは愛していたが，家の機能的要件を妥協することはなかった。まず何よりも，住宅はアートギャラリーではなくて「家」であるべきだ！　第2には，クライアントは私たちに「ビーチとその向こうにある港を望む美しい風景をとにかく最大限活かしてほしい」と強く要望した。私たちは，イサム・ノグチの作品にインスピレーションを求めた。彼のアイコニックな彫刻は曲線を描き，ねじれながら，別世界の入口へと私たちを誘う。

　このコンクリートの彫刻的なフォルムは技術と建築の融合であり，眺望，自然光およびプライバシーの要件に合わせて配置された一連のボックスとして体現されている。陽向き，サーマルマス，そして自然換気についての基本的な設計理念が，デザインの根幹をなしている。

　この住宅とコミュニティをいかに強く結びつけるかという点が，デザインプロセスにおいて重要な局面となった。通常，この地域では道路に面して高いフェンスやインターホンが並んでいるが，私たちは道行く人たちが建物に触れ，建物を通してバルモラル・ビーチの眺望が見えるようにしている。そしてこのような建築経験を更に楽しめるように，厳選された芸術作品をメインの地下室とその先の庭に細心の配慮を払いつつ配置した。鋳造された人型の彫刻がおとなしく横たわり，両腕をいっぱいに伸ばし足先を北へ向けて，誰かが声をかけてくれるのを待っている。最近あったエピソードでは，二人の小さな男の子が通りかかって，一人が「なんで『死んだ人』がいるの？」と尋ねると，もう一人が「あれは『死んだ人』じゃなくて，アートだよ！」と答えていた。

　住宅の内部からの眺望を丁寧に編集しフレーミングすることで，都会的な環境の中において静謐さと隔絶感を生み出している。はめ殺し窓は壁の奥深くに取付けて壁の厚みを見せ，分厚いコンクリート壁をさらに強調している。開閉可能な窓は全て木製サッシとし，隠しレール上でスライドさせる。格納式の可動ルーバーが上部のコンクリートにはめ込まれている。オーストラリアの海岸沿いの生活で直面する自然の猛威に対して，家全体を閉じることもできる。

　この建物の中には，コレクターが生涯を通じて収集してきた彫刻や美術作品がある。それぞれの美術作品の個々の設置条件やロジスティクスなどの要件も，他の居住者の要件と同様に考慮されている。階段自体もコンクリートから彫り出されたような彫刻的なフォルムで，上部からの光に照らされている。トップライトから降りそそぐ光は常に変化し，中に置かれた彫刻作品をより生き生きと感じることができる。

　木とコンクリートのシンプルな組み合わせは，アートコレクションの豊かな色調やテクスチャーと対照的である。建築はシームレスに延長され，室内へと繋がる。メインリビングルームの上部には，目を奪うようなイヴ・クライン・ブルーの天井が浮かんでいる。これと同様に研ぎすまされたデザインのこだわりは，建物のディテールにも顕著に現れている。外壁は意図的に内壁へと変換され，軒裏は天井へと連続する。高さ3.6メートルの扉を全面にわたって引き開けると，キッチンは庭の一部になる。そこは木々の中の巣のような，安息の地が広がっている。

Opening at staircase 階段室の開口部

Staircase 階段

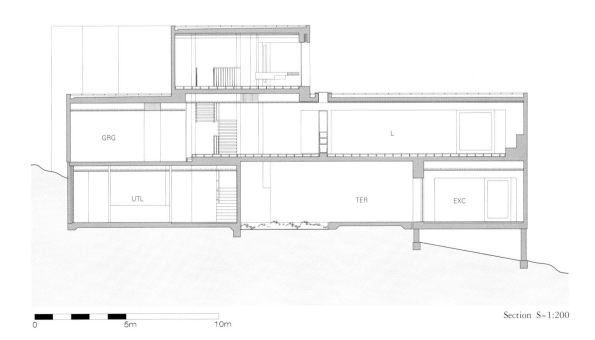
Section S=1:200

Living room: looking northwest 居間：北西を見る

Living room: view toward terrace on northeast 居間：北東のテラスを見る

View from terrace of kitchen (right)　台所（右）のテラスより見る

Kitchen/dining room　台所／食堂

Staircase with skylight on first floor 2階，天窓から光の差し込む階段室

Master bathroom 主浴室

△▷ Master bedroom 主寝室

Bathroom on lower ground floor　地階，洗面室

Lower ground floor　地階 ◁△

Garden room (left) and carport (right) ガーデンルーム（左）とカーポート（右）

DAVID WELSH + CHRISTINE MAJOR
GARDEN PROJECT
Sydney, New South Wales, Australia
Photos: Yoshio Futagawa

Downward view 見下ろし

View toward carport/garage　カーポート／ガレージを見る

Carport　カーポート

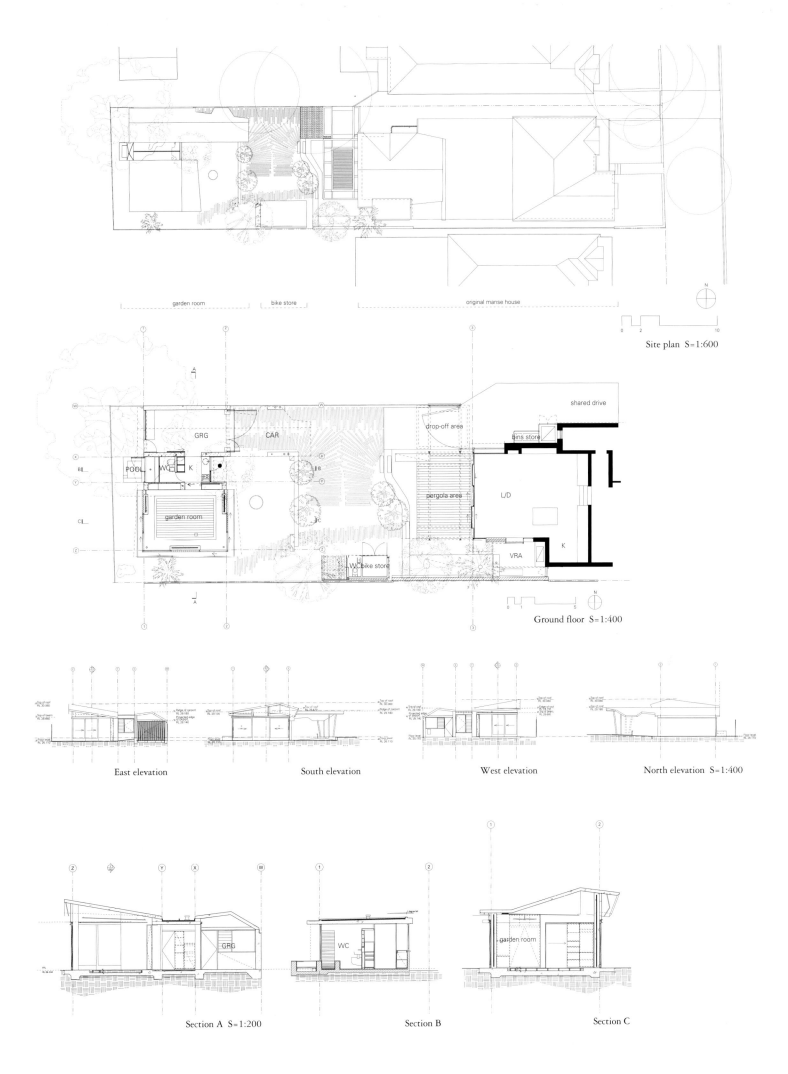

David Welsh + Christine Major / Garden Project

△▽ Garden room ガーデン・ルーム

Garden room: looking south　ガーデン・ルーム：南を見る

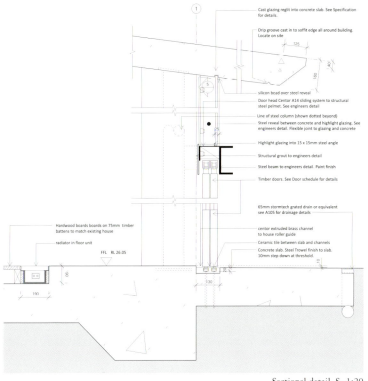

Sectional detail　S=1:20

David Welsh + Christine Major / Garden Project　61

Corner detail 角部詳細

The spaces, connections and uses of rear of a late Victorian home in inner-city Sydney have been re-imagined by creating a flexible series of indoor and outdoor spaces that actively link the original house with its surroundings to transform it into a garden oasis.

The project has the garden at its centre. An in-situ concrete "garden room" sits at the rear of the site to bookend the animated central garden space. Permeable walls are created between internal spaces and garden spaces. Small outdoor areas around the house and the garden room are reclaimed as living spaces and as green backdrops.

Sometimes it is a bedroom, sometimes a study. It can be a self contained, separate living space. It is a garage, except when it is a workshop, or playspace. In the future it might have other uses we have yet to consider....

The new buildings, and the garden itself, are augmentations—they extend the way the original house works for the family who live in it, along with their friends. The built form works as extension of the original house, as a separate entity, or something in-between.

The folded and floating concrete roof creates a sense of both enclosure and lightness; solidity and transparency. The internal spaces are permeable, defined by floor and ceiling planes rather than walls. Robust materials are chosen to take on the patina of the garden itself—concrete walls and roof with timber doors and windows. Unpainted galvanized steel will dull over time to a soft silver reflecting.

As the density of our cities increase, and the pressure on available land rises, this project presents a model not just of best practice environmentally sustainable design (high thermal mass, water capture/reuse, passive solar design principles, and energy efficient fitments) but also one that considers issues of social sustainability. Our houses are getting bigger, however there are less people living in them; the overall demand for, and consumption of, housing and other resources increases in proportion to the number of households rather than to the total population. This trend therefore has significant social and environmental repercussions. Different, flexible housing models need to be considered—our garden project is just one of them....

Garden room: looking north　ガーデン・ルーム：北を見る

Bathroom　洗面室

View toward pond over bathroom　浴室越しに池を見る

View from existing living room. Glazed wall and frames are newly installed by architects　既存の居間より見る。ガラスとフレームは，建築家により新たに加えられた

Pagola newly installed by architects at existing house　既存家屋，建築家により新たに加えられたパーゴラ

View toward driveway from garage　ガレージより車の通路を見る

シドニーの都心部にあるヴィクトリア朝後期の住宅の裏庭スペースを住宅にどうつなげるか，また使い道について再考した。屋内外空間のフレキシブルなつながりをつくることで，この住宅と周辺環境を積極的に結びつけ，この場所を庭のオアシスへと変える。

このプロジェクトの中心には庭がある。現場打ちコンクリート造の「ガーデン・ルーム」が敷地の奥に設けられ，真ん中の生きいきとした庭のブックエンドとなる。透過性のある壁が内部や庭に立てられ，住宅の周りの小さな屋外エリアとガーデン・ルームは，リビングスペースと緑豊かな背景として一新された。

ガーデン・ルームは，あるときは寝室，またあるときは書斎として使われる。必要な設備の整った離れのリビングスペースにもなる。作業場や遊び場でないときは車庫にもなる。将来的には予想外の別の用途もありうるだろう。

この新しい建物と庭全体は，従来の家での暮らし方や友人たちとの過ごし方に広がりをもたらした。新しい建物のかたちは，従来の家の増築部分とも別個の建物とも，あるいはその中間にあるものとしても捉えることができる。

折れ曲がったコンクリート屋根は宙に浮き，包まれている感覚や軽さ，量感や透明性を感じさせる。内部は，壁ではなく床と天井面で規定され，自由に出入りできる。木製のドアと窓を備えたコンクリートの壁や屋根など，庭の趣きにふさわしい存在感のある素材を選んだ。無塗装の亜鉛メッキ鋼は時を経てくすみ，控えめな銀色の輝きを帯びるだろう。

都市の密度が増加し，入手可能な土地に需要が集中する中で，このプロジェクトは環境的なサステイナブルデザインの最良の実施例（高断熱性，集水・再利用水システム，パッシブソーラーデザインの基本原理，省エネルギー設備機器）を提示すると同時に，社会のサステイナビリティについての問題も考慮している。我々の住宅はどんどん大規模になる一方で，そこに住む人数は減っている。住宅や関連物資の全体的な需要と消費は，全人口に対してではなく，住宅戸数に対して増加している。結果的に，この傾向は社会と環境に多大な影響を与えている。従来と異なるフレキシブルな住宅モデルを考える必要があるだろう。このガーデン・プロジェクトはその一例である。

Architects:
Welsh + Major Architects—
Christine Major, David Welsh, principals-in-charge; Steven Sheridan, Gabrielle Pelletier, project team
Consultants:
Birzulis Associates, structural;
Welsh + Major Architects, interior designer;
Peter Fudge Gardens, landscape;
Robert Hannan, arborist; Henry & Hymas, hydraulic
General Contractor: Davden Enterprises
Structural system:
off form concrete walls and floors
Major materials: reinforced in-situ concrete
Site area: 723 m²
Building area: 80 m²
Total floor area: 60 m²
Design: 2010-11
Construction: 2011-13

David Welsh + Christine Major / Garden Project　65

SATOSHI MATSUOKA + YUKI TAMURA
HOUSE ON BACKYARD
Hitachi, Ibaraki, Japan

Photos: Katsumasa Tanaka

View from east 東より見る

Site plan S=1:4000

This house is situated in a compactly structured district where natural setting with ups and downs, multiple main roads, industrial lots peculiar to Hitachi and residential area mix within about 3 kilometers spanning in the east-west direction. Work places are in proximity to residences and a sea breeze can be felt near a mountain when climbing up little higher. Such 'large area with real sense' extends. On the other hand, commercial facilities scatter in residences in the neighborhood and almost half of the land use is occupied by parking. In fact, largest parking lots in the area surround the house on three sides. A point of departure of the plan was to take in 'large area with real sense' into everyday lives through open space of the parking lots.

In order for a family of three to live on about 50 square meters small backyard, simple rectangular rooms are piled up. Living space resulted in narrow pieces in up and down was connected by staircases and voids. Large stair treads are built in the entire staircase and at the same time risers are shifted towards the back, so the whole staircase is as if open to below and is connected to the long side of a rectangle.

The fan-shaped staircase is linked to the main building and adjusts privacy between the two houses, facing the utility zone of the main building. Also, it functions to regulate atmosphere by easing sunshine from the south and catching wind that blows to the east and the west. It resolves problems unique to addition on a 60 meter-long deep-shaped site. On the other hand, rectangular rooms connect to the 'large area' through the open space of large parking lots on the north, and are ruled by the height from the ground, openings and the relation between inner rooms. Though having completely different contexts and sense of scale, the staircase gently covers the rooms like a veil and mutually and mildly permeates the outer space and stacked living space.

Wide treads connect various rooms and space up and down by curves in movement and give variety to rhymes and actions of everyday lives, from places such as a steep ladder to a sunlit loose-stepped terrace. The staircase prepares for tomorrow living scope that bulges out from three-layered square rooms by changing the quality from a staircase to louvers, fixtures around windows and furniture to rely bodies, responding to the depth of treads and different uses in rooms.

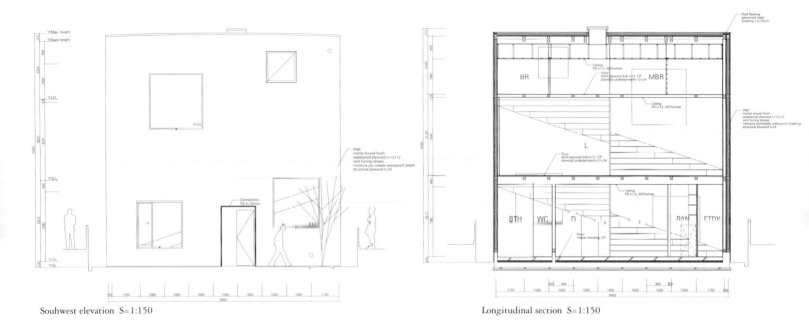

Souhwest elevation S=1:150

Longitudinal section S=1:150

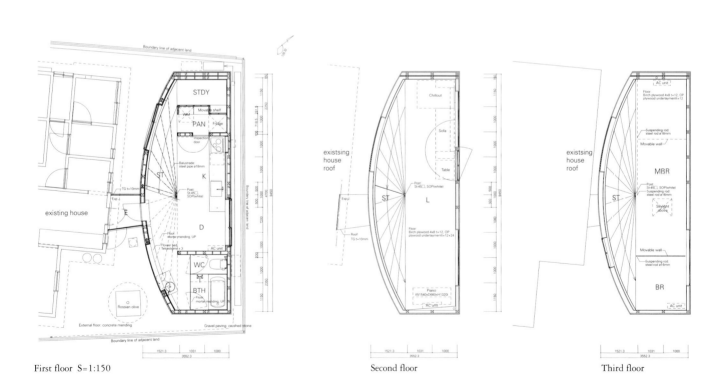

First floor S=1:150

Second floor

Third floor

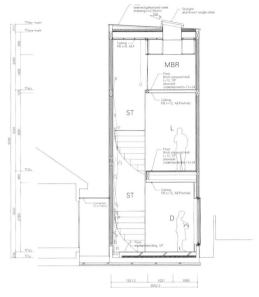

Cross section

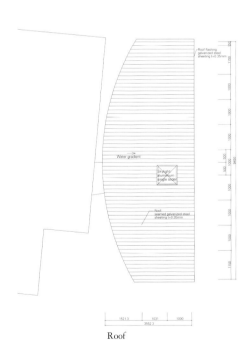

Roof

View from south 南より見る

Satoshi Matsuoka + Yuki Tamura / House on Backyard

Entrance: existing house on left 玄関：左は母屋

Looking southeast from entrance 玄関より南東を見る

Space under staircase 階段下の空間

Architects:
MATSUOKASATOSHITAMURAYUKI—
Satoshi Matsuoka, Yuki Tamura, principals-in-charge; Koh Machida, project team
Consultants:
A.S.Associates—Akira Suzuki, structural; SOLSO, vegetation; Akane Moriyama, fabric
General Contractor: Sokensha
Structural system: wooden
Major materials: mortal trowel finish, exterior; plaster trowel finish, birch plywood, mortar mending, PB, interior
Site area: 608.14 m²
Built area: 30.46 m²
Total floor area: 68.54 m²
Design: 2011-12
Construction: 2012-15

Fan-shaped staircase: dining room on left 扇形の階段：左は食堂

Living room on second floor　2階，居間

Staircase: view from living room　階段：居間より見る

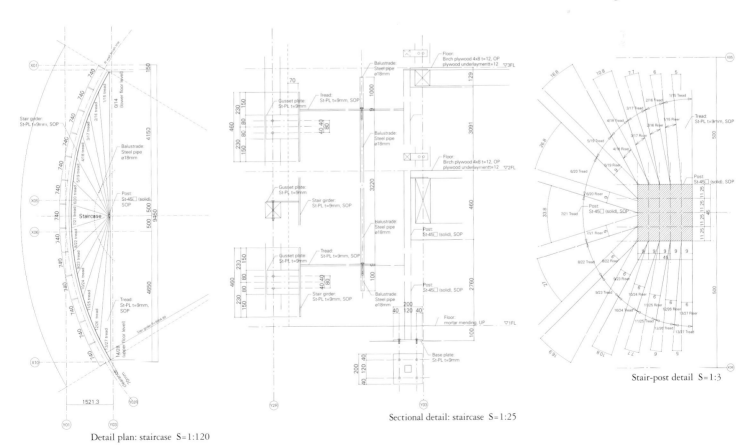

Detail plan: staircase　S=1:120

Sectional detail: staircase　S=1:25

Stair-post detail　S=1:3

Satoshi Matsuoka + Yuki Tamura / House on Backyard

Living room on second floor　2階，居間

　東西約3キロの狭い範囲に，起伏のある自然と複数の幹線交通，日立特有の工場と住宅地が混じりあう，コンパクトな構造をもつエリアにこの住宅は建っている。職住近接で交通の利便性が高く，少し高いところに上ると山を間近に望んで海風を感じる，そんな「実感できる広域」がひろがる。一方，近隣を眺めると住宅に混じって商業施設が点在し，土地利用のほぼ半分が駐車場で占められている。実際，この住宅は近隣で最大の駐車場に三方をとり囲まれている。駐車場というオープンスペースを通して「実感できる広域」を日常に取りこむことが計画の出発点となった。

　15坪ほどの小さな裏庭で家族3人が生活するために，シンプルな矩形平面の居室を積みあげ，結果として上下に細切れになってしまった生活空間を，階段と吹抜けによってつなぎ合わせた。階段室全体に大きな段板が架かり，同時に蹴込板を奥にずらすことで全体が吹抜けであるような階段室が，矩形の長辺に接続されている。

　扇形の階段室は母屋に接続し，母屋のユーティリティ・ゾーンに面して二つの住宅間のプライバシーを調整する。また南からの日射をやわらげ，東西に吹く風をとらえる環境調節の機能をもつ。奥行き60メートルの敷地の，末端の狭い土地での増築で生じる問題を引き受けている。一方，矩形の居室は北に広がる大きな駐車場の明るいオープンスペースを通して広域とつながり，地上からの高さと開口部，そして内部の部屋どうしの関係に支配されている。全く異なるコンテクストとスケール感をもちながら，階段室はヴェールのように居室をやわらかく覆い，外部環境や積層する生活空間をおだやかに浸透させる。

　幅広い段板は，移動のカーブによって上下のさ

Upward view of staircase　階段，見上げ

△▽ Bedroom on third floor　3階，寝室

まざまな部屋やスペースをつなぎ，急なハシゴのようなところから，陽のあたるゆるい段状のテラスのような場所まで，日常の生活のリズムやふるまいを多様なものにする。居室間の使い方の変化に応じて，階段から吹抜けのルーバー，窓周りの調度や身をゆだねる家具へと質を変えながら，3層の四角い居室からはみ出てしまう住むための余地を，この階段室は将来に向けて準備している。

Satoshi Matsuoka + Yuki Tamura / House on Backyard　75

YURI NARUSE + JUN INOKUMA
SPLIT HOUSE
Tokyo, Japan

Photos: Katsumasa Tanaka

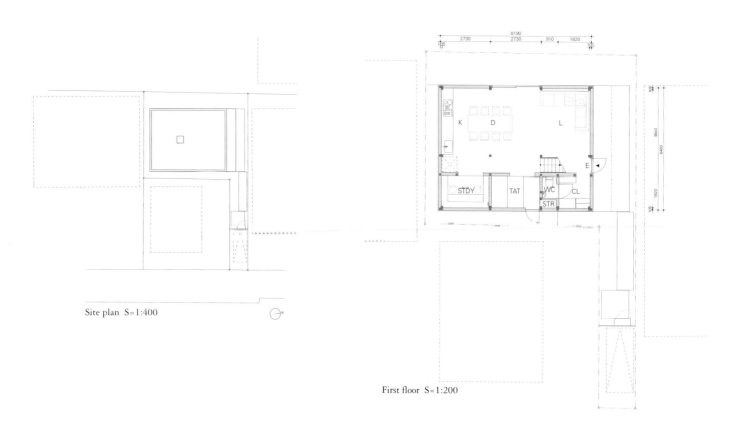

Site plan S=1:400

First floor S=1:200

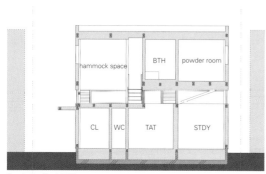
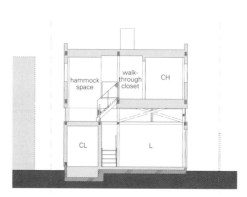

Sections S=1:200

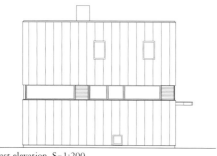

East elevation S=1:200

South elevation

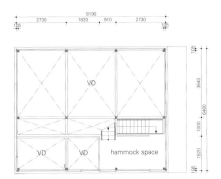

Mezzanine

Second floor

View from approach on east　東側のアプローチより見る

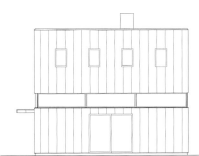

West elevation

North elevation

The house is split into the first and the second floor, provided with a intermediate layer that opens up for 360 degrees in between.

The site in a flagpole shape is located in a crowded district with wooden houses in Tokyo. We chose this composition in order to resolve difficult situation to attain both lighting and privacy and to gain bright and extensive space.

The first floor is spacious space, gathering common-use functions such as kitchen, dining room, sofa space, shared study and tatami room. The second floor houses small private rooms without closet and storage that also functions as a circulation path. Private rooms are minimized and all the functions except for sleeping beds were shared, so that the users of private rooms can be easily changed and the space has redundancy to respond to the change of family menbers flexibly.

Multiple braces were assembled so as to counteract lateral force at the intermediate layer that does not have any structural walls. As a result, the overall building became like a forest, light shining through the structure of branch-like braces to spacious first floor and columns penetrating the small rooms of the second floor where small space continues.

If the purpose was just to split the first and the second floor, it is more honest to build without columns and braces. This time, however, wooden structural bodies were dared visible to give human scale to the large living room and to enjoy the existence of wood as structural and as material. It is a trial to unify practical existence of objects into a spatial configuration, rather than to construct only abstract spatial composition.

First floor: kitchen/dining room/living room　1階, 台所／食堂／居間

Staircase to mezzanine 中2階へ通じる階段

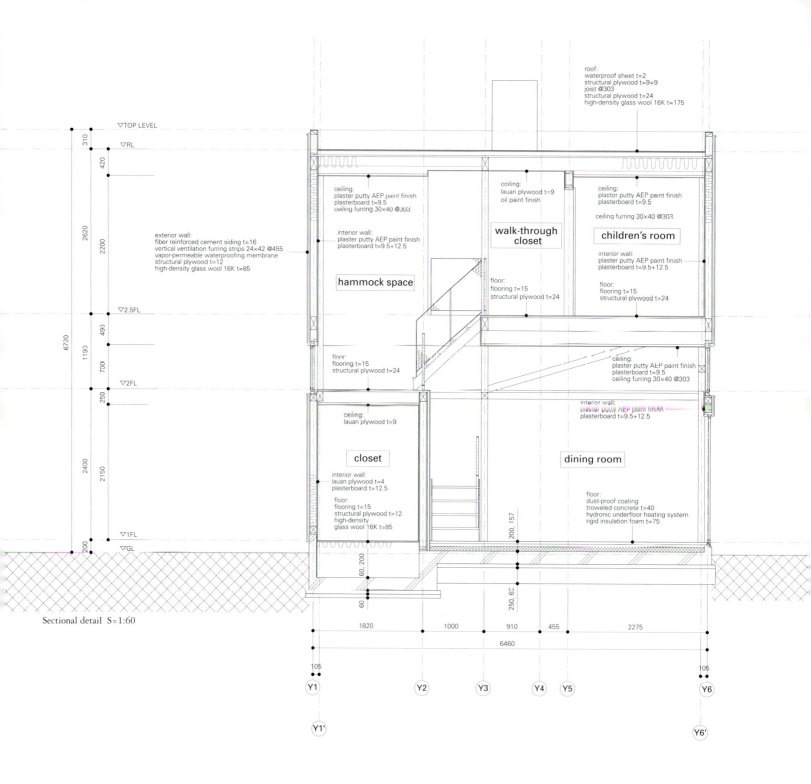

Sectional detail S=1:60

　この住宅は、1階と2階を切り離し、間に360度開口部の中間層を設けた建築である。
　敷地は東京某所、木造住宅が密集する地域の旗竿敷地。採光とプライバシーの両立が極めて困難な状況を打開し、明るく広がりのある空間を獲得するため、この構成を採用した。
　1階はキッチン・ダイニング・ソファスペース・共用書斎・和室など、共用の用途を集めた広々とした空間、2階は収納のない小さな個室と、動線を兼ねた納戸による空間である。個室を最小化し、ベッド以外のすべての用途を共用化することで、個室の利用者を入れ替えやすくし、家族構成の変化に柔軟に対応できる冗長性を与えた。
　構造壁が一切なくなった中間層には、複数のブレースを設けることで、水平力に対応した。結果的に、広々とした1階は枝のようなブレース混じりの構造から光が降り注ぎ、小さな空間が連続する2階は小さな部屋の中に柱が貫く、全体として森のような建築となった。
　1階と2階を切り離すことだけを目的にするならば、柱もブレースも無い方が純粋だ。しかし今回は、あえて木造の構造体を見せることで、広いリビングにヒューマンスケールを与え、構造材・素材として木の存在感を味わうことができる空間をつくり出した。抽象的な空間構成のみを建築化するのではなく、即物的なモノの存在感を、空間構成に統合する試みである。

First floor: looking west　1階：西を見る

First floor: looking east. Tatami room on center　1階：東を見る。中央は和室

Yuri Naruse + Jun Inokuma / Split House　81

Hammock space on mezzanine 中2階，ハンモック・スペース

Walk-through closet leads to each room on second floor
2階，各部屋に通じる納戸

Mezzanine 中2階

Mezzanine with 360 degrees opening　全面開口部の中2階

Architects: Naruse-Inokuma Architects—
Yuri Naruse, Jun Inokuma, principals-in-
charge; Kayoko Ishikawa (ex-staff),
Satoshi Ota, project team
Consultants:
Akira Suzuki/ASA—Yosuke Kimura, struc-
tural; Gn—Masakazu Gokita , Naoko Narita,
mechanical
General Contractor: Kitazawa construction
Structural system: timber
Major materials:
fiber reinforced cement siding, exterior;
plaster putty, AEP paint finish, interior
Site area: 122.42 m²
Building area: 52.90 m²
Total floor area: 105.25 m²
Design: 2013-14
Construction: 2014

Childrens' room on second floor　2階，子供部屋

Salone del Mobile is a furniture fair held annually in Milan (with additional exhibitions on luminaires and workspace on even-numbered years and kitchen and bathroom exhibitions on odd-numbered years). For a stretch of 6 days some 300,000 visitors from around the globe flock to the trade fair, and a variety of events take place in the streets of Milan where the mood is festive. The fairgrounds, being a place of business, only opens its doors to the public the last two days, whereas the streets of Milan is flooded with admission-free events, with independent exhibits by furniture manufacturers who do not participate to the trade fair, as well as exhibits and installations of a wide array of genres. For the past 5 to 6 years, off-site exhibition areas have been expanding at a tremendous rate.

But the furniture industry is full of ups and downs: some brands have moved their shops out from the main street; a brand that showed with much fanfare using a famous architect some years ago had no trace left of their former glories; and the impact of economic downturn seen everywhere. The number of visitors to the trade fair has declined too, drawing 15,000 less than it did last year. Although the area of off-site events is expanding, the number of events appears to be decreasing. As an occasion where design connoisseurs get together, this is the ideal place for a company's public relations activities, but maintaining one's presence here certainly proves to be costly. This year more foreign companies refrained from participating, probably after they have raised enough publicity the previous year.

Nonetheless, Italians are extremely good at creating a jovial atmosphere. Everyday there is a party going on. People with a glass of wine in hand come out into the streets and enjoy a spring night out. It is still an extraordinary all-Italian annual event.

Furniture/Luminaire Designs (Fairgrounds)

Following the autumn 2008 Lehman Brothers collapse, a considerable drop in the number of visitors was observed. But this year 341,721 visitors (including 30,881 non-professionals) traveled to Rho Fiera where the trade fair was held. The figures are smaller than the last year's, but have recovered to the 2008 level. This year saw a significant increase of visitors from Russia, China and most prominently the Middle East. A

Patricia Urquiola: Shimmer mobili/ GLAS ITALIA　パトリシア・ウルキオラ：Shimmer mobili／GLAS ITALIA

MILANO SALONE

Konstantin Grcic: Sam Son/ MAGIS　コンスタンティン・グルチッチ：Sam Son／MAGIS

Ron Arad: Glider/ MOROSO ロン・アラッド：Glider／Moroso

REPORT 2015

Jasper Morrison: Alfi/ emeco ジャスパー・モリソン：Alfi／emeco

ミラノで毎年行われる家具（奇数年は照明器具，オフィス，偶数年はキッチン，バスルームが加わる）の見本市，ミラノサローネ。6日間の期間中にイタリア国内外合わせて30万もの人々が来場することから，それを見込んで市内では様々なイベントが400近くも行われ，ミラノの街は文字通りお祭り状態となる。見本市会場がビジネスの場であり，一般人の入場を最後の2日に限っているのに対して，市内は無料の催しものがほとんどで，また見本市会場に出展しない家具メーカーが独自に展示を行ったり，デザイン関連だけでなく幅広いジャンルの展示／インスタレーションが繰り広げられ，市内展示エリアはここ5，6年でどんどん拡大している。

ただ家具業界の浮き沈みは激しく，目抜き通りに店を構えていたブランドが移転していたり，数年前に有名建築家を起用して華々しくショーを行っていたブランドが見る影もなかったりして，経済の低迷は随所に感じられた。見本市会場の来場者数は，昨年より1万5千人ほど減っている。市内のイベントもエリアは拡大しているが，イベント数自体は昨年より少ないようだ。デザインの目利きが一同に会する場所なので，企業の広報活動としてはうってつけだが，持続するのはコスト的に厳しいのかもしれない。名が知れ渡ったところを見計らってか，今年は参加していない外国企業も目立った。

とはいえ，そんなことを感じさせない盛り上がりを演出するのがイタリア人はとても上手い。毎日どこかでパーティが行われ，ワインを手に人々が道に溢れ出て，楽しそうに明るい春の夜を過ごす。1年に一度の国を挙げたイベントなのは変わりない。

家具／照明デザイン（見本市会場）

2008年秋のリーマンショックを受けて一時来場者数はぐっと落ち込んだものの，今年は34万1,721人（うち一般来場者は3万881人）が見本市会場のロー・フィエラに訪れた。去年より少ないが，2008年程度までには回復している。ロシア，中国はもちろん，今年の特徴としては，中東からの来場者が多かったようだ。ここでは，のべ2,106（家具＋インテリア小物＋照明器具＋オフィス）ものブランドが新作紹介を行い，世界各地からのバイヤーと取引する。クラシックからコンテンポラリーまでをカバーしているといっても，これだけ多くの企業がミラノに継続して集結するのを見ると，家具デザインがイタリア人の広く一般の生活に浸透しているのは，日本の比ではない。世界最大の家具見本市がミラノで開催される理由なのだろう。家具は，ここでは一過性の流行，一部の人間の趣味の世界の話ではないのだ。

全部で21あるパヴィリオンのなかで16号館と20号館に家具デザインの最先端は集まっている。どのブランドもまったくの新作は数点だが，素材や色などマ

Milano Salone Report 2015

total of 2,106 brands (furniture & interior & luminaire & workspace) presented their latest products and negociated with buyers from around the world. Covering all styles from classic to contemporary, the venue draws a great number of companies to Milan on a constant basis—furniture design is widely pervasive in everyday life in Italy, much more than it is in Japan. Hence the reason why the world's largest furniture trade fair is held in Milan. Here, furniture is not about transient fashion nor about taste shared among a small group of people.

Of the 21 pavilions, the most innovative in furniture design can be found at #16 and #20. Most brands showed only a handful of latest releases but plenty of minor updates in materials and colors to bring excitement to the show. This year MOROSO and MAGIS were particularly popular among the attendees. Star designers such as Jasper Morrison, Ron Arad, Phillippe Starck, Patricia Urquiola and Konstantin Grcic were present as always, with their products being fully featured everywhere.

It appears that the Italian design industry always keeps their eyes on Japanese designers. The last 10 years saw the rise of Tokujin Yoshioka and Naoto Fukasawa to success, and the latest addition to the list is nendo. This year 12 companies presented their products, and a large-scale private exhibition was held at the Permanente in the city. Over the course of 2 years between 2014 and 2015 they have released 33 collections and over 100 products. Looking at these 3 Japanese designers we somehow realized what the Italian design industry wants from them—subtle, reserved, yet beautiful forms that are different from theirs. nendo makes their presentation in response to such anticipation, topped with a small dose of surprise. But furniture manufacturers who choose them are more into trends and fashion when compared with their attitudes toward European designers. It will be a challenge for nendo if they will have enough endurance to be able to stay at the forefront 10 years from now.

As usual, reproductions of designs by Modernist giants are popular. Cassina showed a major installation in commemoration of the 50th anniversary of Le Corbusier's death and the 50th anniversary of LC series collection. A limited edition of 90 pieces of LC2 made for Maison La Roche was presented to celebrate

Patricia Urquiola

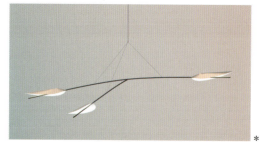

Serena S/ FLOS: LED pendant lamp
Serena S／FLOS：LEDペンダントランプ

Dewey/Kartell: container/bookshelf
Dewey／Kartell：コンテナ／本棚

Serena F/ FLOS: LED standing light
Serena F／FLOS：LEDスタンドライト

Ron Arad

Matrizia/ MOROSO: "the idea came about by accident after seeing mattresses dumped in the street" by Ron Arad
Matrizia／MOROSO：「アイディアはたまたま道に捨てられていたマットを見て浮かんだ」byロン・アラッド

Ettore Sottsass

"Kartell goes Sottsass: A Tribute to Memphis"/ Kartell: two stools and vase (right)
メンフィス・トリビュート／Kartell：二つのスツールと花瓶（右）

Jasper Morrison

Superloon/ Flos: flat disc of LED light rotating 360°
Superloon／FLOS：LEDのフラット・ディスクが360度回転する

Orla/ cappellini

nendo/ Oki Sato

Bison/ cappellini

Float/ MOROSO

Single Curve Stool/ Gebrüder Thonet Vienna

Kurage/ Foscarini: LED light like jellyfish with diffuser of washi paper
クラゲ／Foscarini：クラゲのようなLEDランプ。シェイドは和紙製

Peg/ cappellini: dining table/chair
Pcg／cappellini：ダイニングテーブル／椅子

Ron Gilad

Sfera/ Molteni&C: glass top with three circular steel bases　Sfera（球）／Molteni&C：三つの円形のスティールの上にガラスの天板が載る

Tokujin Yoshioka

Prism/ GLAS ITALIA: glass closet
Prism／GLAS ITALIA：ガラス・クローゼット

Philippe Starck

Ether/FLOS: edge lightng with LED
Ether／FLOS：LEDにより周縁部を照らす

Boxinbox/ GLAS ITALIA: glass shelf
Boxinbox／GLAS ITALIA：ガラスの棚

Big Will/ MAGIS: extending table
Big Will／MAGIS：伸び縮みするテーブル

イナーなアップデートをして、ショーを華々しく盛り上げる。今年はMOROSOとMAGISがとりわけ賑わっていた。ジャスパー・モリソン、ロン・アラッド、フィリップ・スタルク、パトリシア・ウルキオラ、コンスタンティン・グルチッチといったスター・デザイナーは相変わらず健在で、そのプロダクトを全面的に押し出している。

日本人デザイナーの才能に、イタリア・デザイン界がいつも眼を見張っているのも感じられた。ここ10年、吉岡徳仁、深澤直人と来て、今はnendoの活躍が目覚ましい。今年は12社から作品が発表され、市内のペルマネンテ美術館で大規模な個展が開かれた。2014、15年の2年間だけで33コレクション100点以上のプロダクトを世に出したのだそう。この3人の日本人デザイナーを見るとイタリア・デザイン界が彼らに求めているものが浮かび上がってくるような気がする。自分たちとは異なる、繊細で控えめでそれでいて美しいフォルム。nendoはそういった世界からの要望に、ささやかな驚きの物語を添えてプレゼンテーションする。しかし彼らを選ぶ家具メーカーの趣向として、ヨーロッパのデザイナーと比べると流行りすたりがあるようだ。nendoには10年経っても最前線にいられる持続力を持てるかが問われていると思う。

モダニズムの巨匠たちのデザイン復刻も相変わらず多い。Cassinaは、コルビュジエ没後50年、LCシリーズコレクションの50周年を記念して、大々的なインスタレーションを行った。ラ・ロッシュ邸のためにつくられたLC2を、完成後90年にちなんで90点限定で発表。くるくる廻るLC4（シェーズ・ロング）やLC7が、デュリーニ通りのショップのショーウィンドゥを飾り、見本市会場ではミニチュア版が展示された。またKartellは、2007年に亡くなったエットーレ・ソットサスのプロダクトをフィーチャー。コルビュジエとシャルロット・ペリアンの作品をリプロダクトしている照明メーカーのNEMOは、市内のショップで展覧会を行った。アイリーン・グレイの復刻を続けてきたClassiConは、今年、テーブルE1027をマットブラックのフレームで発表している。売り手としても買い手としても評価が定まった名作に対する信頼感は強いのだ。

照明デザインは、LED光源が急増中で、光源を小さくできることからデザインもさらに多様化が進んでいる。間接照明やいくつかの光源をまとめて群として見せるデザインが目立つ。一見すると白熱球のように見えるLEDも多々あり、スター・デザイナーであるインゴ・マウラーは東芝マテリアルが開発したLED光源でLucelino（羽の生えた電球）を再製作した。Artemide、FLOS、FontanaArteといった老舗ブランドはもちろん多くの人を集めていたが、VIBIA、davide groppi、FOSCARINIといった後発ブラ

Milano Salone Report 2015　87

the 90th anniversary of its creation. The rotating LC4 (Chaise Longue) and LC7 decorated their shop on Via Durini, and miniature versions were shown at the trade fair. Kartell featured products by Ettore Sottsass who died in 2007. The luminaire manufacturer NEMO put on an exhibition at their shop in the city, showing reproductions of Le Corbusier and Charlotte Perriand pieces. ClassiCon who has been reproducing Eileen Gray's released the matte black frame version of her table E1027 this year. A strong sense of trust for masterpieces with established values are shared among both sellers and buyers.

Luminaire design is experiencing a boom of LED light: the possibility to diminish the size of the light source brought about the diversification of design. One prominent type of design was the clustering of multiple light sources and indirect lights. LED light bulbs looking similar to incandescent bulbs were also popular: the star designer Ingo Maurer used the LED light developed by Toshiba Material (Lucelino). Long standing brands such as Artemide, FLOS and FontanaArte drew wide attention as per usual, but emerging brands such as VIBIA, davide groppi and FOSCARINI were also building up their presence. VIBIA is a Spanish luminaire manufacturer with a distinguishing clean-cut design using small light sources. davide groppi, like Ingo Maurer, is a brand that bears the name of its designer, with interesting artistic luminaires. The long-established manufacturer FLOS had Ron Gilad design their booth. Ron Gilad is an up-and-coming designer who creates unique abstract products combining contrasting motifs such as plane material v. wire material and mass v. void, mostly working for Molteni&C. FLOS is a brand which demonstrates strong commitments to designers such as Jasper Morrison. Their collaboration with Ron Gilad raises much anticipation.

Exhibitions/Events (Fuori Salone)

Fuori Salone means "outside the salone." In addition to the city's south-western Tortona area near Porta Genova Station, Brera area embracing the Brera Museum, Lambrate area on northeast, Spazio Rossana Orlandi on west, and the University of Milan are now accommodating off-site events.

INTERNI Magazine who publishes Fuori Salone's event index holds the biggest main event every year. This year they showed an exhibition around the theme 'Energy for Creativity' at two different venues, on the University of Milan campus and in the Botanical garden behind the Brera Museum. The theme is certainly a reference to 'Feeding the Planet, Energy for Life', theme for Expo Milano, opening on May 1st this year. At the University of Milan, Kengo Kuma showed his kitchen system IRORI in collaboration with kitchenhouse. Two belt-shaped sheets of vulcanized paper (fiber material such as cotton pulp dipped in zinc chloride solution, laminated, then washed to remove the zinc chloride solution and dried) are twisted and crossed. The intersection is pinned to create semicircular parts that are placed side by side to build a cocoon-like pavilion. Vulcanized paper is similar to plastic at touch but looks like Japanese paper as it transmits light. Inside, a kitchen unit is arranged using laminated bamboo and steel pipes. Kuma has been a regular at Fuori Salone events for the last 10 years, gathering attention with presentations that always make use of technologies and materials that are reminiscent of Japan. While with each year more events tend to opt for easier options, his presence is a valuable one.

Because exhibitors are subject to preliminary reviews and expensive booth charges, many companies, especially the foreign brands chose to exhibit off-site. Dutch Piet Hein Eek held a private exhibition at Spazio Rossana Orlandi, a former tie factory converted to an exhibition space for vintage and modern furniture that is a highlight of Fuori Salone. Piet Hein Eek is known for his furniture that uses waste materials, but this year we saw him tackling new challenges such as sheet copper luminaire. In Brera area, the unique presence of Bolognese manufacturer Viabizzuno stands out. Its president Mario Nanni talks passionately about the way the blue hue in LED can be minimized and the development of devices needed to do so. Often working in collaboration with architects such as Peter Zumthor and Kengo Kuma, his installation consists of lighting inside 7 silos, proposing luminaire design that integrates space.

As for Japanese brands, AGC Asahi Glass experienced their first exhibition at Superstudio Piu in Tortona area. They displayed their specially processed glass that can be applied as projection screen. Young

Zaha Hadid

Aria/ SLAMP: chandelier of 50 transparent surfaces with LED lights positined on their axis
Aria／SLAMP：シャンデリア。50枚の透明なプレートとその軸線をLED光源が照らす

Davide Groppi

Simbiosi/ davide groppi: LED lights connecting with very thin wire
Simbiosi／davide groppi：非常に細いワイヤでつながれたLEDランプ

Ingo Maurer

Prototypes/ Ingo Maurer: light souce positioned on edge of flat shade (right)
プロトタイプ／Ingo Maurer；右はフラットなプレート状シェイドの先端に光源がある

Diego Fortunato

Mayfair/ VIBIA

Ross Lovegrove

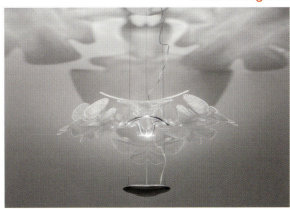

Chlorophilia/ Artemide: body of LED light source as a heatsink with three transparent elements like leaves above　Chlorophilia／Artemide：LED光源のベースが放熱体となり上の葉のような三枚の透明のパーツを照らす

Girgio Biscaro

HollyG/ FontanaArte: LED table light
HollyG／FontanaArte：LEDテーブルランプ

Antoni Arola

Flamingo/ VIBIA: separating LED light source from shade to the bar at bottom
Flamingo／VIBIA：LED光源はシェイドから離れて下のバーにある

Issey Miyake

Wuni (left)/ Artemide: new product of IN-EI collection
Wuni（ウニ，左）／Artemide：IN-EIシリーズ新作

Naoto Fukasawa

Athena/ Artemide: LED standing light
Athena／Artemide：LEDスタンドライト

Le Corbusier

LC VII (Applique de Marseille)/ NEMO: light for Unite d'Habitation, Marseille. NEMO reproducts the masterpieces of Le Corbusier and Ch. Perriand
LC VII／NEMO：マルセイユのユニテ・ダビタシオンのために制作されたランプ。NEMOは，コルビュジエ，シャルロット・ペリアンの照明器具を多く復刻している

ンドも存在感を増していた。VIBIAはスペインの照明メーカーで，小さな光源を使った端整なデザインが特徴。davide groppiは，インゴ・マウラーのようにデザイナーの名を冠したブランドで，オブジェのような照明機器が興味深かった。老舗FLOSでは，ロン・ジラードがブースをデザイン。ロン・ジラードは近年注目のデザイナーで，面材と線材，塊と空といった対照的なモチーフを組み合わせて抽象的でユニークな作品をつくり，多くをMolteni&Cから発表している。FLOSはジャスパー・モリソンをはじめ，デザイナーとの深いコミットメントが感じられるブランドで，今後のロン・ジラードとのコラボレーションも期待したい。

エキジビション／イベント（フオーリ・サローネ）

フオーリ・サローネとは「サローネの外」の意味。市内南西，ポルタ・ジェノバ駅周辺のトルトーナ地区に加えて，近年はブレラ美術館のあるブレラ地区，北東に位置するランブラーテ地区，西側のスパツィオ・ロッサーナ・オルランディ，ミラノ大学など，市内各所に広がりを見せている。

これらフオーリ・サローネのイベント・インデックスを発行している雑誌『インテルニ』は，毎年目玉となるイベントを主催。今年はミラノ大学構内とブレア美術館裏の植物園の2カ所で，「創造にエネルギーを」とのテーマで展覧会が開かれた。これは今年5月1日から開かれるミラノ万博のテーマ「地球に食料を，生命にエネルギーを」になぞらえたものだろう。ミラノ大学では隈研吾がキッチンハウスとコラボレーションしてキッチンのシステム「IRORI」を展示した。帯状にしたバルカナイズド・ペーパー（コットンパルプなどからつくられた原料を塩化亜鉛溶液に浸して積層した後，塩化亜鉛溶液を除去し乾燥させた素材）2枚をひねりつつ交差させ，交点をピンで留めて半円形のパーツをつくり，それを並べて繭のようなパヴィリオンをつくった。バルカナイズド・ペーパーはプラスティックのような手触りだが，光を透過し見たところ和紙のようでもある。その中には，竹の集成材と鉄パイプによるキッチンユニットが提案された。隈はこの10年間，フオーリ・サローネのイベントによく登場しているが，いつも日本を意識させる技術，素材を使ってプレゼンテーションし，人々の注目を集めている。午々安易な方に向かっている感のあるイベント群の中で貴重な存在に映る。

見本市会場は出展料が高く審査もあることから，特に外国企業は市内で展示を行うブランドも多い。オランダのピエト・ヘイン・イークはスパツィオ・ロッサーナ・オルランディで個展を開いた。ここは古いネクタイ工場を改装して，ヴィンテージものや現代の家具を展示しているスペースで，フオーリ・サローネでも注目すべき場所。ピエト・ヘイン・イ

Japanese architect unit ARTEN-VARCH was in charge of the exhibit design. AGC has been increasing their outlets in Europe, and their glass was used for Parisian train windows. In that sense, releasing their latest products on this occasion in Milan will prove to be extremely effective.

Louis Vuitton showed travel-inspired artistic pieces under the theme 'Objets Nomades' by 9 designers such as nendo, Patricia Urquiola and Campana Brothers at Palazzo Bocconi. Each exhibition room demonstrated a different taste—for example a Louis Vuitton trunk and a hammock arranged in a jungle. Charlotte Perriand's project La Maison au Bord de L'Eau (1934), unrealized, was realized along with its furniture. A high-budget project that attracted many visitors who appreciated its cost and enjoyed its visuals.

Shoes brand UNITED NUDE presented shoes created by 5 designers using 3D printers, produced by Rem Koolhaas who has a famous architect uncle with the same name. Zaha Hadid's shoes were stunningly beautiful. Her name is listed at the Salone del Mobile every year without fail. This year her wall-hanging objets and table were shown at CITCO, door handle at OLIVARI and chandelier at SLAMP and WORLDGLASS. Even small-scaled designs that are not architecture do justice to her strength in creating forms.

There were also food events, probably in time with the opening of Expo Milano that takes place on May 1st. Lexus' 'Journey of the Senses' exhibit, alongside their cars on display, offered food to stimulate our senses. It was one of the most popular exhibit.

Overall, many events are often amateurish and opportunistic, but we always take pleasure in finding out the few exceptional exhibits that can only be seen at this timing. Accumulation of such experiences definitely creates an uplifting feeling that proves to be highly inspiring for those who design as well as for those who enjoy design.

text/photos by Hitomi Saito except where specified
* courtesy of respective companies

nendo/ Oki Sato

"nendo works 2014-2015": exhibition with over 100 works of 33 collections, 19 brands in these two years
"nendo works 2014-2015"：この２年間に19ブランド，33コレクションから発表された計100以上の作品が展示された

AGC

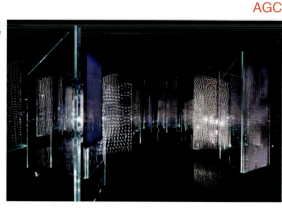

"Glacier Formation": exhibition of new product Glascene which allows images to be projected onto transparet glass.
Installationed by ARTENVARCH.
"Glacier Formation"：映像投影できる透明ガラスの新製品「Glascene」の紹介。
空間デザインはアーテンバーク

Mario Nanni/ Viabizzuno

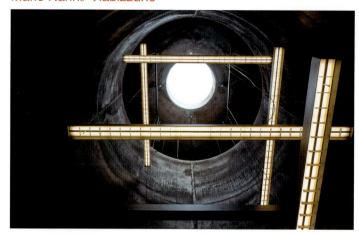

"solis silos": installation showing new n55 light bulb with 7 silos. Viabizzuno directed by Mario Nanni is unique manufacturer pursuing integration of space and lighting design
"solis silos"：七つのサイロを使って行われた新作n55 ライトバルブのインスタレーション。
マリオ・ナンニ率いるヴィアビッズーノは建築家のコラボレーションが多く、空間と一体化した照明デザインを提案するユニークなブランド

United Nude

Zaha Hadid	Ross Lovegrove	Ben van Berkel

"Re-Inventing Shoes": five architects designing high heels using 3D printing techonology. United Nude is directed by Rem Koolhaas as same as his famous uncle's name
"靴の再・発明"展：5人の建築家が3Dプリンターを使用してハイヒールをデザイン。ディレクターのレム・コールハースは同名の著名なおじを持つ

Kengo Kuma

"IRORI" and "White Cocoon" produced by kitchenhouse: INTERNI's exhibition "Energy for Creativity" at Univ.of Milan. Kitchen with laminated bamboo and steel pipe; pavilion with 1 mm-thick vulcanized paper twisted and crossed
「IRORI」「繭」produced by kitchenhouse：ミラノ大学構内で開かれたインテルニ誌主催「Energy for Creativity 2015」展の一つ。竹の集成材と鉄パイプでつくられたキッチンと、1ミリ厚のバルカナイズド・ペーパーをひねり2枚を交差させて強度を持たせたパヴィリオン

Louis Vuitton

"Objets Nomades": 9 designers' travel-inspired objects; supended chair by Campana Brothers (left) and light by nendo (right)
「オブジェ・ノマド」：9人のデザイナーの提案する、旅をインスパイアするオブジェ。カンパナ・ブラザーズによるぶら下がりチェア（左）とnendoによる携帯ライト（右）

Piet Hein Eek

New products displayed at Spazio Rossana Orlandi with designer himself
スパツィオ・ロッサーナ・オルランディで開かれたピエト・ヘイン・イークの個展。座っているのはデザイナー本人

ークは廃材を使った家具で知られているが、今年は銅板の照明器具など新機軸のものが見られた。ブレラ地区では、イタリア、ボローニャのメーカーViabizzunoの展示がユニークな存在だろう。代表のマリオ・ナンニは、LEDのブルー味をいかに抑えるか、そのための器具開発について熱く語る。ピーター・ズントーや隈研吾など建築家とのコラボレーションも多く、空間と一体化した照明デザインを提案し、今年はサイロを七つ並べその内部で照明のインスタレーションを行った。

日本のブランドは、AGC旭硝子がトルトーナ地区スーパースタジオ・ピューで初出展。映像の投影が可能な、特殊加工が施されたガラスを展示。会場デザインは日本の若手ユニット、アーテンパークが担当した。AGCはヨーロッパでも販路を拡大しており、パリの電車の窓ガラスなどでも採用されている。その意味では、この時期ミラノで新作発表するのはとても効果的だろう。

ルイ・ヴィトンはパラッツォ・ボッコーニで「オブジェ・ノマド」と題し、nendoやパトリシア・ウルキオラ、カンパナ・ブラザーズといったデザイナー9名が、革を使った〈旅をインスパイアする〉オブジェを提案。ジャングルの中に置かれたルイ・ヴィトンのトランクとハンモックなど、各部屋ごとに趣向を凝らした展示がされていた。またシャルロット・ペリアンの実現しなかったプロジェクト「水辺の家」（La Maison au Bord de L'Eau、1934年）を家具と共に制作。資金を掛けた企画展で、それは来場者にも伝わる。多くの人が訪れ、見て楽しい展覧会だった。

靴のブランド、UNITED NUDEは、5人のデザイナーによる3Dプリンターを使った靴を発表。プロデューサーはレム・コールハースで、同じ名前の著名建築家をおじに持つ。ザハ・ハディドの靴が美しかった。彼女の名前はミラノ・サローネでは毎年必ず登場する。今年は、CITCOから壁掛け式のオブジェやテーブル、OLIVARIからドア・ハンドル、SLAMP、WORLDGLASSでもシャンデリアが展示されていた。建築ではない小さなスケールのものでも彼女の造形力は十分に発揮されている。

5月1日に始まるミラノ万博に合わせてなのか、食の関連のイベントもあった。レクサスは「五感を巡る旅」と称して、車の展示の他に五感を刺激する食を提供。大変人気なポイントだった。

機に乗じた感のある学芸会的なイベントが数多いのだが、その中からこのタイミングでないと見られないような好展示を見つけ出すのは楽しいことでもある。そういったものの集積が生み出す高揚感は、デザインする者にとってもデザインを享受する者にとっても、かなりな刺激であることは間違いない。

（文／写真（特記ない限り）：斎藤日登美）
＊各社提供

ANDRÉS CASILLAS & EVOLVA ARCHITECTS
MEXICAN CONTEMPORARY HOUSE
Melbourne, Victoria, Australia
Photos: Yoshio Futagawa

View from street 道路より見る

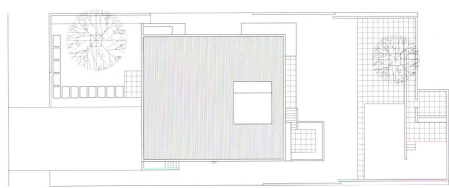

Site plan

First floor

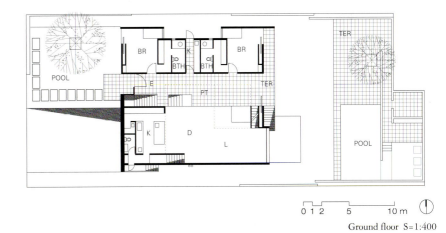

Ground floor S=1:400

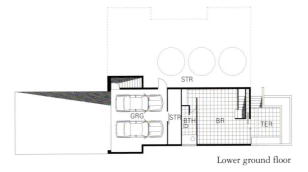

Lower ground floor

Andrés Casillas & Evolva Architects / Mexican Contemporary House

Garden elevation 庭面

Swimming pool　スイミング・プール

Pond 池

Entrance 玄関

Andrés Casillas & Evolva Architects / Mexican Contemporary House　97

The brief was to deliver a contemporary Mexican modernist house, designed by Mexican architect Andrés Casillas, in an unremarkable residential street in Melbourne, Australia. The site has an east west orientation and flat topography in a medium density suburban context. The clear challenges were to create a sense of privacy, a feeling of space and to bring sunlight into the house.

Andrés Casillas is widely acknowledged as Luis Barragán's only protégé and collaborated with Luis Barragán on his famous house, *Cuadra San Cristóbal*. His design of the Melbourne project skilfully checks all the boxes, providing a house, characteristic of his oeuvre, and one that pays homage to Barragán's core principle of expressing serenity.

To deliver the house, thirteen and a half thousand kilometres away from Mexico, presented other challenges. The client sought a sympathetic local architect and engaged Evolva Architects, an emerging Melbourne practice with its own connections to Mexico underpinning an understanding of the essence of Casillas' design. Evolva took on the responsibility of developing the design, documentation and administration of the project.

Competing demands of privacy and sunlight were resolved through the adoption of a centuries old Spanish quadrangular layout, where the functions of the house revolve around a central courtyard—the Central Patio. Direct sunlight fills this enclosed central space via a soaring clerestory and as a result, through doors and opening panels, light filters into all the rooms.

The spaces contract and release—the 2.1 meters high entry transitions to a 5.0 meters high interior. Narrow, hidden stairs ascend to secreted bedrooms and studios. Grand cruciform shadows track their way across towering off-form concrete walls.

Stairs to living/dining room　居間／食堂への階段

Unexpected apertures pierce stairway walls and high corners, bringing into play a careful orchestration of space and natural light.

The house turns its back on the adjoining properties and directs its focus inward. A vast picture window looks east towards the rear garden. This combination of spatial arrangement and framed views creates not only a sense of seclusion but also a sense of remoteness from the outside world despite its urban surroundings. The oasis of garden and pool, surrounded by high walls, conveys a monastic sense of tranquillity and an illusion of solitude.

Encountering the house in the street is dramatic—it is the embodiment of the enigmatic facade. Monumental and understated, it evokes beauty in its visual economy. Brutalism, inherent in the expanse of off form concrete is tempered by the animation of shadows from trees and reflections from water. A moment spent in contemplation of the facade reveals a surprising gentleness; a subtleness and softness in its addition to the street.

Matthew Scully/Evolva Architects

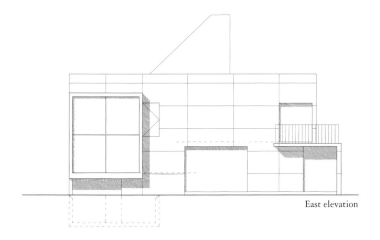
East elevation

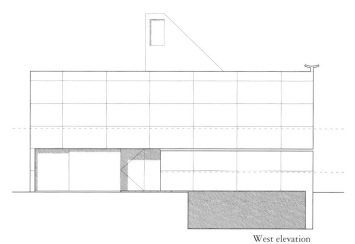
West elevation

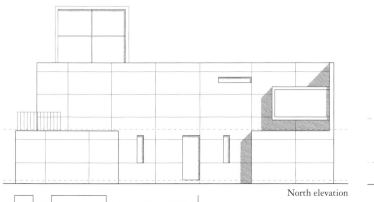
North elevation

South elevation S=1:200

North-south section S=1:200

Andrés Casillas & Evolva Architects / Mexican Contemporary House

Living/dining room 居間／食堂

Architects:
Andrés Casillas & Evolva Architects—
Andrés Casillas, Matthew Scully (Evolva Architects), principals-in-charge
Client: Andrew and Victoria Greensmith
Consultants:
Clive Steele Partners, structural;
Evolva Architects, interior designer;
greenscene, landscape;
John Armsby-Energy Solutions, energy consultant
General Contractor: Delft Constructions
Structural system:
off form concrete walls and floors
Major materials: concrete
Site area: 770 m^2
Building area: 254 m^2
Total floor area: 420 m^2
Design: 2008-12
Construction: 2012-14

Living/dining room　居間

　メキシコの建築家，アンドレス・カシージャスがオーストラリア・メルボルンのごく一般的な住宅街に設計したメキシコのモダニズム住宅の概要を紹介する。敷地は東西方向に長く，中程度の密度の郊外の平坦な土地に位置する。このプロジェクトの明らかな課題は，プライバシーが守られ，かつ広がりのある空間をつくること，そして住宅内に自然光を取り込むことだった。
　アンドレス・カシージャスはルイス・バラガンの唯一の弟子であり，バラガンの有名な「サン・クリストバルの厩舎」の協力設計者として広く知られている。メルボルンのプロジェクトにおける彼のデザインは，住宅をつくる上でのすべての条件を巧みに満たしており，また彼の作品の特徴である「静けさ」の表現は，バラガンの基本理念に敬意を表している。
　13,500キロも離れたメキシコから住宅を実現させるにあたって，様々な問題に直面した。クライアントはよき協力者となる地元建築家を捜し求め，メルボルンを拠点とする設計事務所，エヴォルヴァ・アーキテクツを起用した。メキシコとの独自の繋がりを持つ我々は，カシージャスのデザインの本質を理解し，実現をサポートし，このプロジェクトの実施設計，設計図書作成および監理を担当した。
　クライアントの要望に応えてプライバシーと自然光を確保するために，1世紀前のスペインの住宅の四角形の配置に倣って，家の中心にある中庭──セントラル・パティオ──の周囲に住宅の各機能を配置した。閉じられた中央の空間は直射光で満たされ，その光は高窓，ドアや開閉式パネルの開口部を通過して，すべての居室に届けられる。
　空間は収縮，拡張して，天井高さ2.1メートルのエントランス部分から5.0メートルの高さのある室内空間まで変化する。内包された狭い階段を上がると，隠れ家のような寝室とスタジオがある。荘厳な十字形の影が，高くそびえる打放しコンクリート壁を横切っていく。階段の壁や隅部の高い部分など，思いがけない所に開口部が穿たれており，差し込む光と空間が繊細に響き合っている。
　この住宅は隣接する土地には背を向け，内側に向かっている。大きなピクチャー・ウィンドウが東側の裏庭に向かって開かれている。この空間構成とフレーミングされた眺望が相まって，隔絶された雰囲気と同時に，都会的な環境にもかかわらず外界から遠く離れているような感覚を与える。高い壁に囲まれた庭園とプールのオアシスは，修道院にいるような静寂な感覚，そして孤独な幻想を呼び起こす。
　通りからこの住宅を見ると，謎めいたファサードの存在感はドラマチックだ。モニュメンタルでありつつも控えめなファサードは，その抑制された視覚効果が美しさを生んでいる。ブルータリズムの特徴である打放しコンクリートは，揺れ動く木々の陰影や水面の反射によって和らげられている。このファサードがもたらす黙想のひとときは思いがけず優しく，街路に繊細さと柔らかさを添えている。
（マシュー・スカリー／エヴォルヴァ・アーキテクツ）

Living room: staircase (right) to master bedroom 居間：主寝室への階段（右）

View toward dining room from living room: staircase (left) to studio 居間より食堂を見る：仕事部屋への階段（左）

Upper part of staircase from living room to master bedroom: reflection of pink door on wall　居間からの主寝室へ続く階段上部：壁にはピンクの扉の影

Corridor to master bedroom　主寝室への廊下

Master bedroom　主寝室

Bathroom　浴室

Window of master bedroom 主寝室の窓

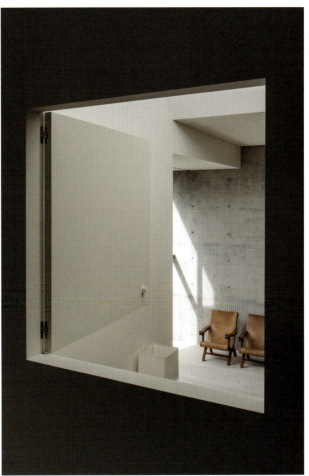

Window of master bedroom 主寝室の窓

View toward studio from master bedroom
主寝室より仕事部屋を見る

Studio 仕事部屋

YUTAKA YOSHIDA
HOUSE IN KAITA
Hiroshima, Japan

Photos: Katsumasa Tanaka

Site plan S=1:2000

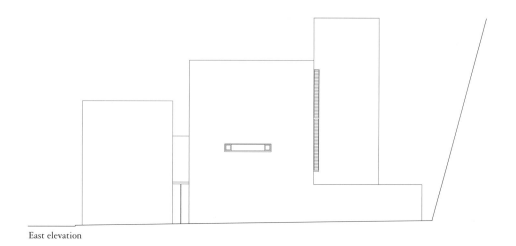

East elevation

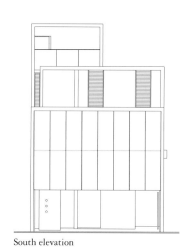

South elevation

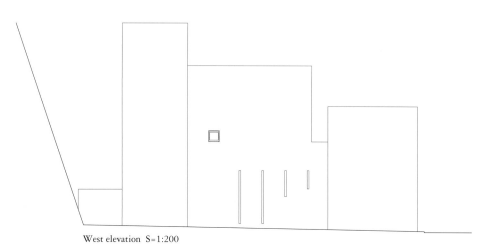

West elevation S=1:200

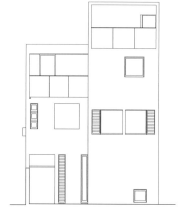

North elevation

View from south 南より見る

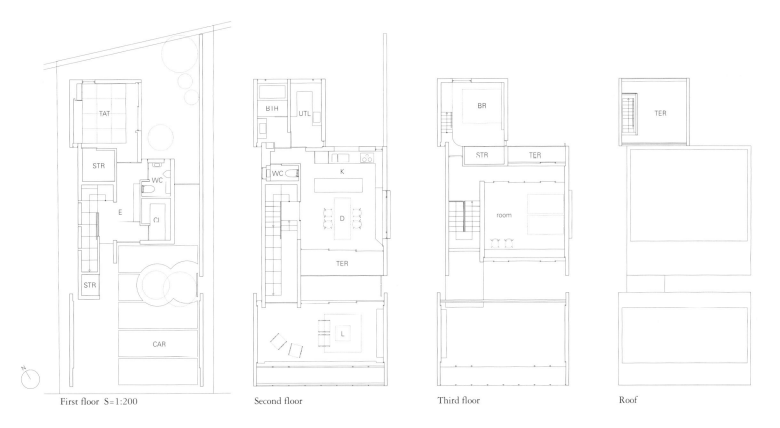

First floor S=1:200

Second floor

Third floor

Roof

Yutaka Yoshida / House in Kaita

Evening view from south 南側夕景

East elevation 東面

Plants at gap of living room and dining room above
上部の居間と食堂の間のスペースに植えられた草木

View from garage. Living room above　ガレージより外を見る。上は居間

Gap between expanded metal facade (left) and living room (right)
エキスパンドメタルによるファサード（左）と居間（右）との隙間

Entrance　玄関

Staircase with natural light from slit
階段：スリットから光が差し込む

Staircase from entrance to living room and dining room
玄関から居間と食堂へ続く階段

Tatami room　和室

Architects:
Yutaka Yoshida Architect & Associates—
Yutaka Yoshida, project team
Consultants: Kaneko Structural Engineers—
Takeshi Kaneko, structural; Design-room
Taniguchi—Masaharu Taniguchi,
Nishikawa Architecture Equipment Design—
Minoru Nishikawa, mechanical
General Contractor:
Shoda Construction Co., Ltd.
Structural system: concrete, steel frame
Major materials: concrete, gypsum board
Site area: 156.63 m^2
Built area: 93.72 m^2
Total floor area: 218.35 m^2
Design: 2012-13
Construction: 2013-14

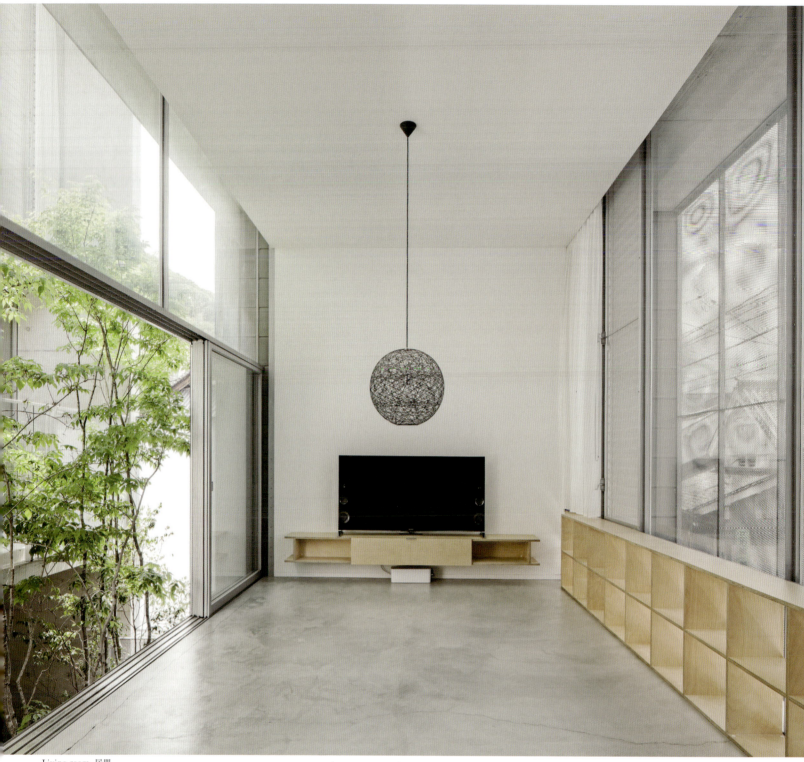

Living room 居間

Wooden houses are dotted on both sides of a narrow road and old remnant streetscape still remains in the neighborhood, which used to be one of the post towns along Sanyodo—a main road running through Sanyo region, west part of the main land—in Edo period. The site is located at the bottom of a cliff on the north side, where a temple is situated on its top and the shape is long and narrow in the south-north direction. Therefore, we considered it is important to fit scale sense to the post town at the frontal road side and to avoid oppressive feeling toward the cityscape on the exterior that can be seen from a vacant lot beside the site.

The plan is composed with a two-story steel building on the road side that has a possibility of enlarging the width, and a combination of three- and four-story reinforced concrete building on the back. Making gaps between each building and shifting the plan in order to lead lighting and ventilation in, each room faces outer air and the others through buffer area.

Main spaces located on the second floor are positioned in distance such as living room in the two-story building and dining room in the three-story building, and tunnel-like corridor connects them. In this way, each room has slight level difference, so as to create diagonally crossing view and the atmosphere of large volume inside. Especially, it commands a extensive view of the first to the third floor through buffer area at living room with 3.4-meters-ceiling-height.

Living room: view through expanded metal screen
居間：エキスパンドメタル・スクリーン越しに外を見る

Corridor to dining room from living room　居間と食堂をつなぐ廊下

The light look of extrusion-molded plate at the steel part and the monolithic look of concrete are combined and create a mixed material look on the side elevations, which usually become one large wall. Also, the facade made of expanded metal that controls gaze from outside and lets light in gives a new appearance in the cityscape with wooden lattices.
Yutaka Yoshida

Circulation: staircase to bedroom above　動線部：上階の寝室へ続く階段

Buffer area between living room (left) and dining room (right)　居間（左）と食堂（右）の間の緩衝スペース

Opening between dining room and staircase　食堂入口の開口部

Living room: view toward dining room through buffer area　居間：緩衝スペース越しに食堂方向を見る

Dining room: view toward living room　食堂：居間方向を見る

Bathroom (left) and utility room (right) 浴室（左）と家事室（右）

かつて江戸時代に山陽道の宿場町の一つであった周辺には，幅員の狭い道路の両脇に，木造家屋が点在し，当時の面影漂う街並が今も残っている。敷地は，北側の山頂部に寺を構える裏山の崖下にあり，南北に細長い。そのため，前面道路に対しては，宿場町にスケール感を合わせつつ，敷地脇の空地から見える外観においては，街並に対して圧迫感を持たせないことが肝要であると考えた。

ここでは，将来幅員の広がる可能性のある計画道路側には鉄骨造による2層の棟，その奥に鉄筋コンクリート造による3層と4層を組み合わせた棟から成る構成を採用した。そこに，採光や通風の確保のため，棟毎に平面的にずれや隙間を設けながら，それぞれが外気に有効に接し，また外気を挟みながら向き合う諸室関係をつくり出した。

2階に設けた主たる生活スペースは，リビング

Sections S=1:200

を2層棟に，ダイニングは3層棟にと，離して配置し，トンネル状の動線空間で繋いだ。こうして対峙する室は，床レベルを僅かにずらすことで，斜めに交錯する視線を生み，内部に大きな視覚の気積をつくり出している。とりわけ，3.4メートルの天井高さを持つリビングからは，外気を挟みながら1階から3階までを含む大きな視界が開かれる。

鉄骨部の軽やかな押出成型板の表情と，そしてコンクリート部のモノリシックな表情を組み合わせ，大きな1枚壁になりがちな側面ファサードに異なる素材の混在した表情を生み出し，視線を制御しながら光を通すエキスパンドメタルによるファサードが，木製格子の点在する街並に新しい表情を与えている。

(吉田 豊)

Terrace テラス

Staircase to bedroom 寝室へ続く階段

Bedroom: staircase to terrace on left 寝室：左はテラスへ続く階段

CASEY BROWN
PACIFIC HOUSE
Palm Beach, Sydney, New South Wales, Australia

Photos: Yoshio Futagawa

Overall view from north 北側全景

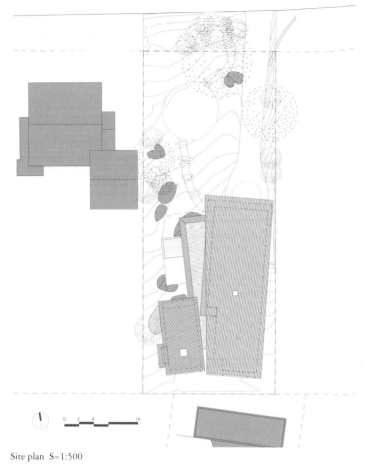

Site plan S=1:500

Approach アプローチ

Clad in dramatic burnt timber, and the ochre tones of weathered steel sheets, this holiday house is sure to satisfy the family's brief for a beautiful house taking full advantage of the natural features of the site.

The main living areas of the house soar out towards the panoramic water views, giving the house a dynamic and striking appearance. Large expanses of glass to the north capture the spectacular views to the Pacific Ocean, Palm Beach and the Barrenjoey Light House.

An existing weatherboard cottage on the site created an exciting siting opportunity. Rather than locating the new house at the lower point of the site, it breaks the pattern of the street, sitting high and away from any neighbours, giving a strong sense of privacy and retreat.

The house is split into two pavilions, linked by a deck which expands and fans out to the view. The first pavilion contains the living spaces, kitchen, family bathroom and bedrooms, with a casual living area at the lower level adjacent to the small plunge pool. A hidden door into the second pavilion reveals the master bedroom suite, which sits among the treetops, overlooking the swimming pool and northerly view. The main living area is light and spacious, contrasting with the modest scale of the bedrooms.

Key to the design is the idea of the family being together in these living spaces, entertaining and relaxing with family and friends. From the main living area, a large expanse of stacking glass paneled doors slide away to seamlessly connect the indoors with the outdoor deck.

The entry to the house is via a steep path and sandstone steps, which take you upon arrival underneath the dramatic cantilever of the living space. This luminescent space glows with the rich reds, oranges and browns of the weathered steel. A single Y-shaped column, delicately formed and tapered supports the house above.

The upper levels are clad in charred

Architects: Casey Brown Architecture—
Robert Brown, principal-in-charge;
Carly Martin, project team
Consultants:
Murtagh Bond—Ken Murtagh, structural;
Hugh Burnett, landscape
General Contractor: John Newton
Structural system:
masonry and concrete (lower level),
steel and timber structure (upper level)
Major materials: timber, weathered steel
cladding, concrete, timber flooring
Site area: 836 m²
Building area: 250 m²
Total floor area: 250 m²
Design: 2011-13
Construction: 2013-14

Lower ground floor   Ground floor S=1:400

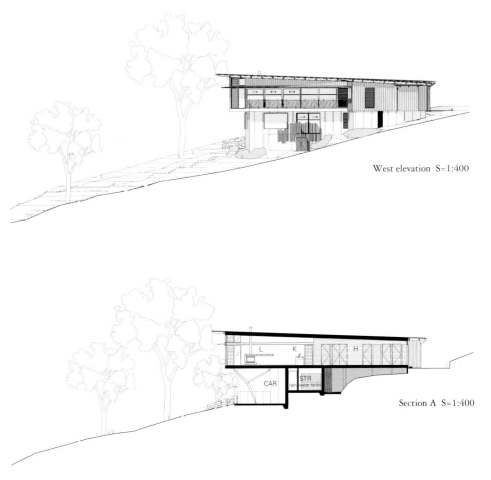

West elevation S=1:400

Section A S=1:400

black vertical boarding, burnt using the traditional Japanese Yaki-Sugi method. Treating the boards in this way seasons and helps protect the otherwise vulnerable wood. The timber acquires a unique charred texture, not dissimilar to the patternation of crocodile skin. The palette of colours used for the house, from the oranges to the reds, browns and blacks, resonates with the Australian landscape.

A place for retreat, relaxing, entertaining and gathering—this special house captures the view, sun and breezes to create a memorable holiday home highly suited to the unique opportunities of the site.

Entrance 玄関

Detail of structure 構造ディテール

122

View from west 西より見る

Casey Brown / Pacific House 123

Deck: living/dining room (left) and master bedroom (right)　デッキ：居間／食堂（左）と主寝室（右）

印象的な焼板，そして耐候性スティールのオークル系の色彩に包まれたこの別荘は，「敷地の自然を最大限活かした美しい家」という施主一家の要望に確実に応えている。

この住宅のメイン・リビングエリアは海景のパノラマに向かって舞い上がるように伸び，ダイナミックで印象的な外観を呈している。北側の大きなガラス面からは，太平洋，パーム・ビーチ，そしてバレンジョイ灯台の素晴らしい眺望が広がる。

敷地にあった下見板張りの小屋が，配置を決定する上で面白いきっかけを与えてくれた。新しい住宅を敷地のより低い地点に配置するのではなく，近隣の家々から離して高い地点に配置することで町並みのパターンを崩し，プライベートな隠れ家としての性格を強めている。

この住宅は二つのパヴィリオンに分かれており，それらは眺望に向かって扇形に広がるデッキで繋がれている。一つめのパヴィリオンにはリビングスペース，キッチン，家族のバスルームおよび寝室が設けられており，下階には小さなプランジプールとその横にカジュアルなリビングエリアが備えられている。二つめのパヴィリオンに繋がる隠し扉を入ると，木々の緑に囲まれた主寝室が現れ，そこからはスイミング・プールと北側の風景を望むことができる。寝室の控えめなスケール感とは対照的に，メイン・リビングエリアは明るく広々としている。

△▽ Pool room　プール・ルーム

　設計にあたって重視したのは，一家がこれらのリビングスペースで一緒に過ごし，家族や友人たちと楽しみ，リラックスするということだ。メイン・リビングエリアは，一面に広がるガラスパネルのドアを引き開けると，室内と外部デッキがシームレスに繋がる。

　急傾斜の小道と砂岩でできた階段を辿ると，リビングスペースを支える印象的なキャンティレバーの下に，住宅への入口がある。この空間は，耐候性スティールの赤・オレンジ・茶色の豊かな彩りを映して輝いている。繊細に形づくられテーパーのかかった1本のY字形の柱が，上部の住宅を支えている。

　上の階の外壁は，日本の伝統的な焼杉工法を用いた黒い焼板の縦張りによる。この方法で木板を表面加工することで，痛みやすい木材を乾燥させ保護している。木材は独特な炭化のテクスチャーを帯びており，ワニ皮のパターンと似ているようにも見える。この住宅に用いた色彩は，オレンジから赤のグラデーション，茶色，黒などで，オーストラリアの風景と響き合っている。

　日常から離れてゆっくりくつろぎ，楽しみ，人と集まる場所。眺望・太陽・風を取り込んで，この場所の独自の恵みを満喫でき，思い出に残る休暇を過ごせる特別な家を実現した。

Casey Brown / Pacific House　125

Living/dining room 居間／食堂

Window at kitchen 食堂脇の窓

Fireplace 暖炉

Living/dining room 居間／食堂

Staircase 階段

Brass railings of staircase 階段の真鍮の手摺り

Deck: looking north デッキ：北を見る

Master bedroom: wall by "Yaki-Sugi" methods 主寝室：「焼杉」板の壁

Bathroom 浴室

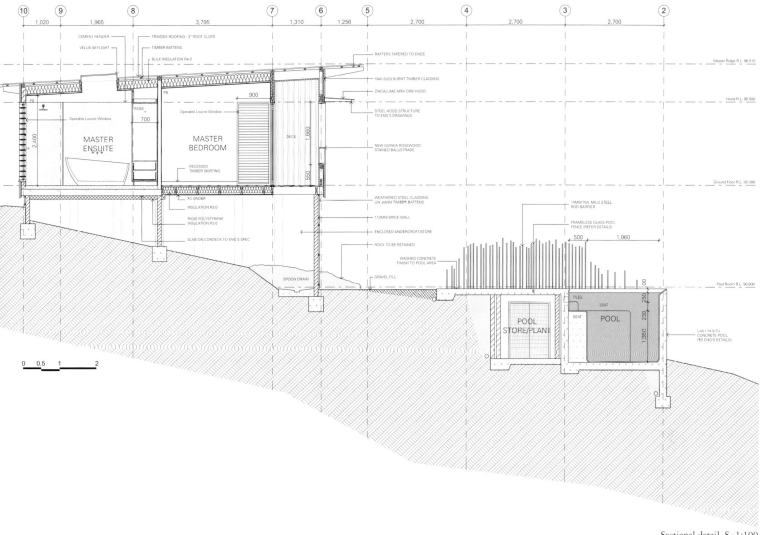

Sectional detail S=1:100

Master bedroom 主寝室

Casey Brown / Pacific House

CASEY BROWN
BARRENJOEY HOUSE
Palm Beach, New South Wales, Australia
Photos: Yoshio Futagawa

Distant view from beach 遠景：ビーチより見る

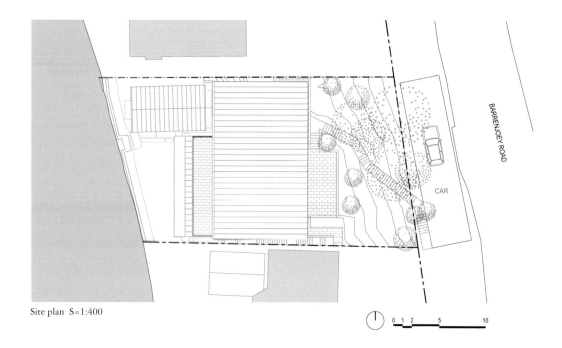
Site plan S=1:400

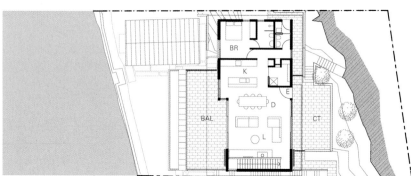
Upper floor

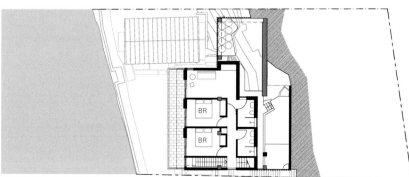
Middle floor

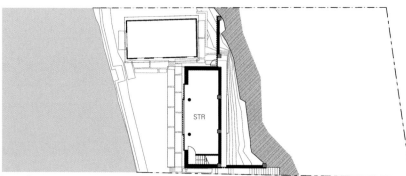
Lower floor

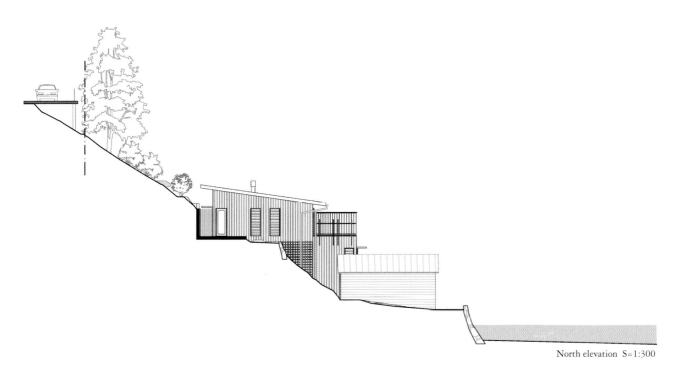

North elevation S=1:300

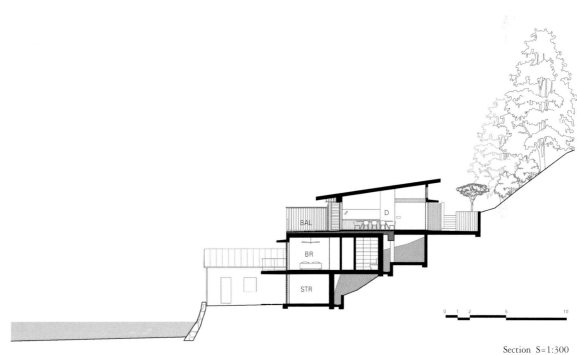

Section S=1:300

Architects: Casey Brown Architecture—
Robert Brown, principal-in-charge;
Toshio Ozaki, project team
Consultants:
Murtagh Bond, structural
General Contractor: Gray Built
Structural system: reinforced concrete, steel
Major materials: zinc, timber (blackbutt), concrete, basalt
Site area: 556 m^2
Building area: 165 m^2
Total floor area: 246 m^2
Design: 2012-13
Construction: 2013-14

View from east 東より見る

Court 前庭

Entrance 玄関

This project is located on the steep shores of Pittwater facing Ku-ring-gai Chase National Park. The project involved the retention of the structural portions of a 1940s beach cottage as well as the parking platform, existing established gardens and boat shed. The objective of the design was to create a series of simple and pleasant spaces where families and friends can gather and to minimise the maintenance required in a long term through the life of the house.

The new additions enclosed the retained structure including the concrete slab and the 6 meters high concrete columns which supported the original cottage. The existing

Living room: court on left 居間：左は前庭

concrete columns required underpinning in order to be retained as the main structural element for the new house. Integrated under the original concrete slab were two new levels, carefully placed into the steep rocky slope and one level above the slab.

This grounded the new building and turned the unused and visually unsightly under croft into usable space allowing the extensions not to be any higher than the original cottage. The new spaces in the under croft was separated from the sloping site by continuous drainage area keeping the house dry at all times though the house is located at the bottom of the hill and exposed to mass of water travelling down the hill. The drainage areas also enable easy access to the back of the house for maintenance purposes where all the services and rain water tanks are installed.

The new building with a lean to zinc roof and native hard wood vertical boarding is a simple functional and easy to maintain beach house with panoramic views from every room while providing a generous sense of space that the original building lacked. Designed with outdoor space to the east and west the house opens up to the light, breeze and views while protecting the occupants from excessive sun and winds.

The exterior timber cladding is left unfinished to weather eventually to natural grey while internal timber elements are oiled to retain its freshly milled surface colour. The original columns were ground and left exposed as the reminiscence of the original beach cottage in the new house. A group of skilled crafts persons were called in by the builder, in order to put together the materials in a sensible manner for this project.

Living room: view toward water 居間：水辺を見る

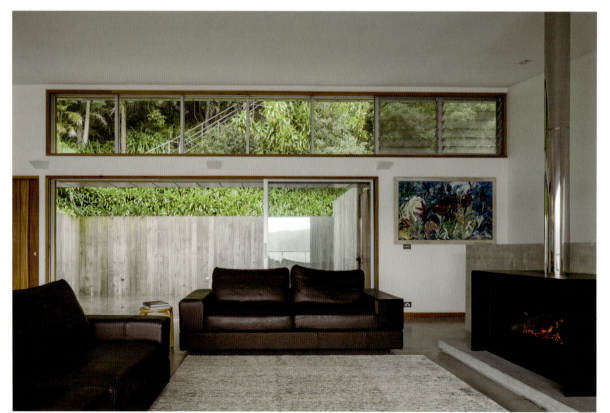
Living room: looking east 居間：東を見る

Dining room/kitchen 食堂／台所

Balcony バルコニー

Casey Brown / Barrenjoey House 139

Kitchen 台所

Staircase 階段

Bedroom 寝室

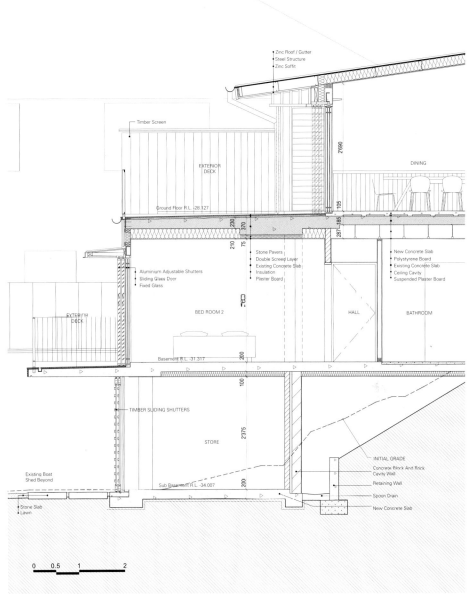

Sectional detail S=1:80

　敷地は，クーリンガイ・チェイス国立公園の切り立った海岸に位置する。計画には，1940年代に建てられたビーチ・コテージ，駐車場，既存の造園された庭，ボート小屋の保存と維持が含まれていた。設計の目的は，家族や友人が集えるシンプルで快適な空間を実現すること，そして住宅の一生を通して長期的に求められるメンテナンスを最小限に抑えることだった。

　既存のコンクリートスラブとビーチ・コテージを支える高さ6メートルの柱を含む構造体はそのまま残し，新しい増築部分で覆われた。既存のコンクリート柱を新しい住宅の主要構造部として維持するためには土台の補強が必要だった。既存のコンクリートスラブの下には新たに2層が組み込まれ，急勾配の岩肌の斜面に慎重に挿入された。もう一層は既存スラブの上に設けられている。

　これによって新しい建築物を固定し，使用されていなかった見映えの悪い地下室を使用可能な空間に転換させたことにより，増築部分を既存のコテージよりも高くならないように抑えることができた。この住宅は丘陵地の底部にあり，丘を流れ落ちてくる大量の水にさらされていたが，連続する排水エリアを設けて，この地下室内の新しい空間を敷地の斜面から切り離すことで，建物は常時乾いた状態を保っている。また，これらの排水エリアを設けたことにより，メンテナンス時には，すべての設備および雨水槽が設置されている住宅の裏側にアクセスしやすくなった。

　新しい建物は亜鉛メッキスティールの差掛屋根と地元産の堅木の縦板張り仕上げで，シンプルで機能的，かつメンテナンスが容易なビーチハウスとなっている。すべての部屋からパノラマの眺望が楽しめると同時に，元の建物にはなかった広々とした空間である。東側と西側には屋外スペースが設けられ，住人たちを激しい直射光や突風から守りつつ，自然光，風，そして眺望に対して開かれた住宅を実現した。

　木製の外装材は無塗装のままで，徐々に風化して自然に灰色になることが想定されている。一方で，室内の木製部材はオイルペイントにして，削りたての木肌の色を保つようにした。既存の柱は固定されて元の姿のまま露出されており，新しい住宅のなかに元のビーチ・コテージの記憶を留めている。施工者は腕の立つ職人チームを呼び，彼らはこのプロジェクトに合う理にかなった方法で材料を組み上げた。

Casey Brown / Barrenjoey House　141

MAKOTO TAKEI + CHIE NABESHIMA / TNA
BETWEEN NATSUMEZAKA
Tokyo, Japan
Photos: Yoshio Futagawa

◁ Bird's-eye view from east 東側上空より見る

View from east 東より見る

Site plan S=1:1500

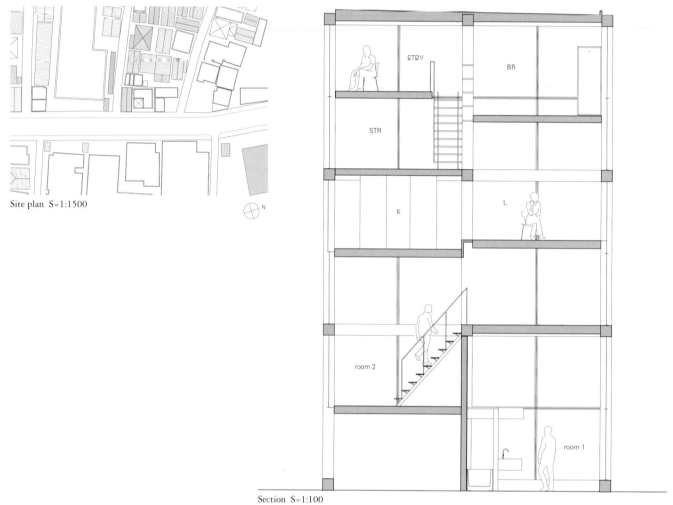

Section S=1:100

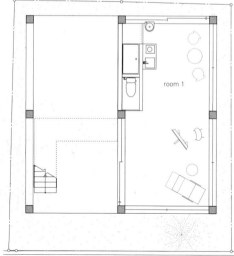

First floor S=1:150

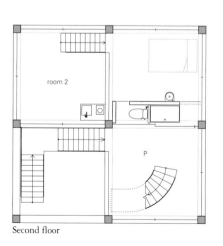

Second floor

Entrance court: room 1 on right　エントランス・コート：右はルーム1

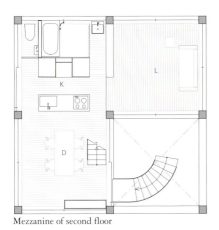

Mezzanine of second floor

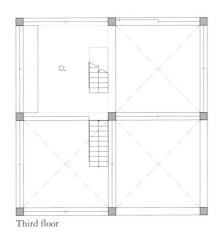

Third floor

Fourth floor

Room 1 ルーム1

Room 2 ルーム2

The site is located in the middle of a hill called Natsumezaka, where the famous Japanese novelist Natsume Soseki's family home used to be situated. Almost half of the site has been designated as part of the future road widening project. The current landscape is defined by apartment complexes consisting of a high-rise building placed behind a two-tiered low-rise, in a composition that anticipates the future road expansion.

We tried to imagine a place that remains constant in this ever-shifting urban environment. Our goal was to create a building that bridges the gap between the new and changed environment and the familiar—a house that maintains its relationship with the hill, neighborhood and the city, even when a portion of the structure is reduced in size and the site is partially turned into a new road.

Cubic frames are layered within the blank space that lies in the middle of the hill, creating an accumulation of spaces, or *ma*. Placed inside these spaces are floors that can be finished at various heights. A high-level floor functions as a bedroom with extensive views, and a floor that connects to the street is a terrace for the rental properties that simultaneously functions as an approach into the main house. These floors, floating at different levels, create various relationships and distances with the surrounding neighborhood.

This building removes the boundaries between public/private such as the house premises-to-urban road and rental areas-to-main house; high/low such as the pillars-to-beams and higher-to-lower floors; and indoors/outdoors such as the rooms-to-balcony and ceilings-to-eaves. This structure, where relationships are not bound to a master-and-servant relationship, is both a classic and contemporary space or *ma* in the city of Tokyo. The project illustrates the possibilities of layered architecture that creates new landscapes by embracing the ever-evolving city as a whole.

Makoto Takei + Chie Nabeshima

Entrance stairs: view toward room 1　エントランスの階段：ルーム1方向を見る

Room 2: downward view from second floor　ルーム2：2階より見下ろす

Entrance porch on mezzanine of second floor 中2階，エントランス・ポーチ

Entrance porch: looking east　エントランス・ポーチ：東を見る

Dining room/kitchen: steel frames with mortar resin coating 食堂／台所。モルタルで被覆されたスティールの構造柱

View from kitchen toward dining room　台所より食堂を見る

　敷地は夏目漱石の実家があった夏目坂という坂道のちょうど中間あたりにある。敷地のほぼ半分は都市計画道路に指定されており，2階建ての低層部分と外壁がセットバックした高層部分をもつマンションが，拡幅される道路幅を暗示しながら街並をつくっている。

　この変化し続ける都市環境の中で，ずっと変わることのない居場所を考えてみる。将来，建物の一部が減築され，敷地の一部が道路になった後も，街や坂や隣家との関係をそのまま保ちながら，新しい周辺環境をより身近に感じる建築をつくろうと考えた。

　坂の途中の大きな余白の中に立方体のフレームを重ねる。そして敷地に積まれた「間」をつくる。その間に自由な高さに設えることのできる床を引掛けた。高いところにある床は眺めの良い展望台としての寝室であり，道路に繋がっている床は母屋へのアプローチを兼ねた賃貸のテラスとなっている。そうやっていろいろな高さに浮いた床はさまざまな距離を保ちながら街と繋がる。

　この建築は，敷地と都市計画道路，賃貸と母屋といった公私，柱と梁，階数といった上下，部屋とバルコニー，天井と庇といった内外の境界を消していく。主従の無い関係が集まってできた建築は，東京という街の古くて新しい「間」なのである。夏目坂の間は，移りゆくありのままの都市を包含しながら，街並を新たにつくり出す積層建築の可能性を示している。

（武井　誠＋鍋島千恵）

Architects:
Makoto Takei + Chie Nabeshima/TNA—
Makoto Takei, Chie Nabeshima, principals-in-charge; Yuki Shioiri, project team
Consultants:
Konishi Structural Engineers—
Yasutaka Konishi, Noboru Enshu, structural-
General Contractor:
Idotekken Construction Corp.—
Kosei Ido, Masaru Hiwatashi
Structural system: steel
Major materials: double-layered glass, resin mortar, solid wood flooring (oak)
Site area: 89.41 m²
Building area: 56.85 m²
Total floor area: 162.86 m²
Design: 2013-14
Construction: 2014-15

Living room 居間

Stairs from dining room to storage and study above
食堂より納戸，書斎へ続く階段

Study 書斎

Study: view toward bedroom　書斎：寝室を見る

Bedroom　寝室

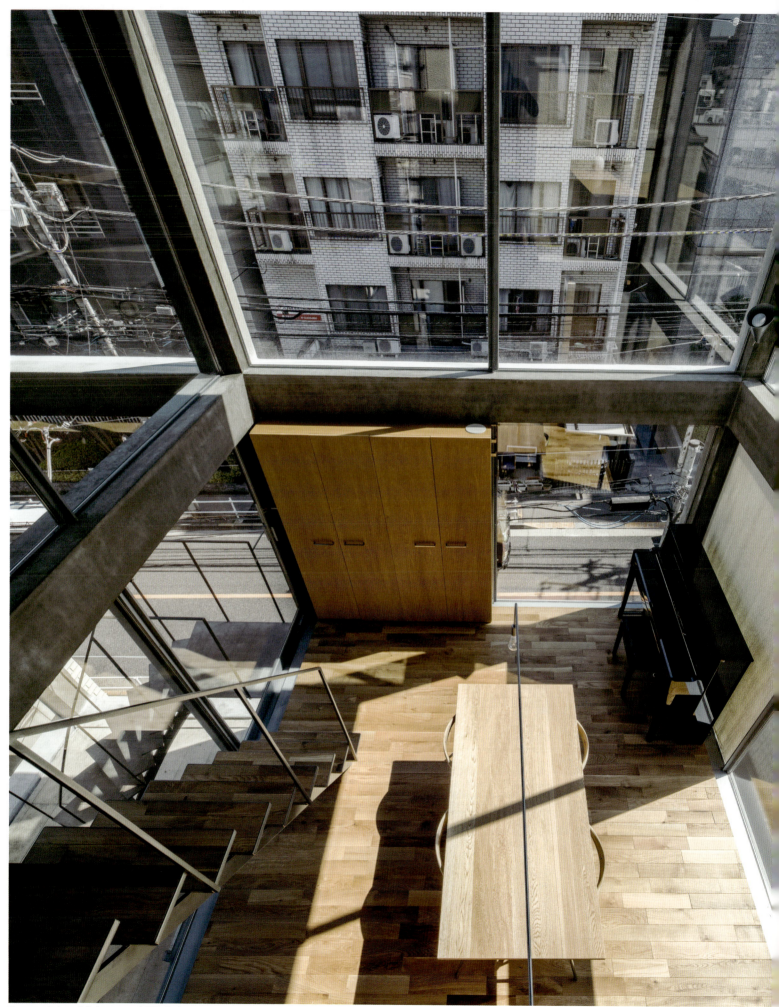

Downward view of dining room 食堂見下ろし

Terrace テラス

GA ARCHITECT 5
ZAHA M. HADID

In 1983, Zaha Hadid made brilliant debut by winning first prize at the competition of "The Peak" in Hong Kong. This project was never realized and she was called the "Queen of the Unbuilt" at that time. However, her distinctive drawings were full of energy which indicated her future success. GA ARCHITECT 05 ZAHA HADID includes 9 projects in her early days. Her drawings are reproduced with high definition and displayed in beautiful layout. The preface is written by Arata Isozaki, who discovered her talent at the competition of "The Peak". This monumental book is a must to know the first stage of the master of contemporary architecture.

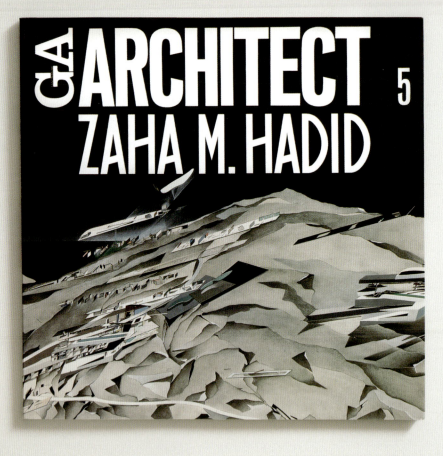

Essay: A Style Acting of Itself: The Architecture of Zaha Hadid / Arata Isozaki; Post-Peak Conversations with Zaha Hadid: 1983 & 1986 / Alvin Boyarsky
Works: Malevich's Tectonik; Museum of the Nineteenth Century; Dutch Parliament Extension; Residence for the Irish Prime Minister; 59 Eaton Place; Trafalgar Square Grand Buildings Project; Parc de La Villette; The Peak; The World

116 total pages / English and Japanese text / Size: 300×307mm　¥4,200+tax

ZAHA HADID
Exhibition "ZAHA HADID" OFFICIAL BOOK

The official book of Zaha Hadid's first large-scale solo exhibition in Japan being held from October 2014. This catalogue covers Zaha's past and present works and reveals how her architecture has developed through time: the vigorous drawings in the days of the "Queen of the unbuilt", the rare works/projects in Japan such as the Moon Soon restaurant in Hokkaido, the major works established her impregnable position as a top architect, and the latest works that draw the global attention such as New National Stadium of Japan. Included works are not limited to architectural field but product design like tableware, shoes and furniture as well. Two of valuable interviews with Zaha (republished) and the essay on their architectural approach by Patrik Schumacher, Zaha's right-hand man, are also contained. This book presents an overview of Zaha's ideas and activities.

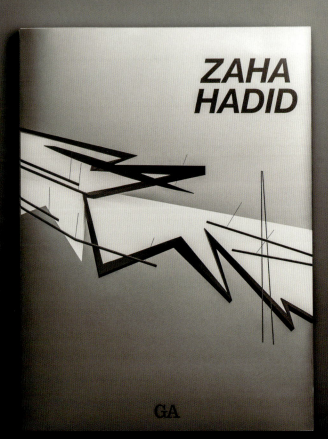

Interview: Interview 1995; Interview 2007 / Zaha Hadid
Essay: The Instrumentality of Appearances in the Pursuit of a Legible Urban Order / Patrik Schumacher
Works: The Peak; The World (89 Degrees); Tomigaya Building; Azabu Jyuban Building; KMR, Art and Media Park; Moon soon; Vitra Fire Station; Cardiff Bay Opera House; Rosenthal Center for Contemporary Art; MAXXI: National Museum of XXI Century Arts; Phaeno Science Center; London Aquatics Centre; Heydar Aliyev Center; Dongdaemun Design Park; New National Stadium of Japan; and others
Products: Crevasse Vase & Niche; WMF Cutlery; Melissa Shoes; Orchis; Lacoste Shoes; and others

236 total pages / English and Japanese text / Size: 300×224mm　¥2,800+tax

GA Contemporary Architecture

For the past forty years, our basic attitude has remained the same. On-site reportages from around the world have amassed a vast collection of architectural works. For this brand-new series of publication, masterpieces of contemporary architecture would be selected from our extensive archives to be classified into various types of building such as museum, library, theater, university, school, and sports, office, etc. A compilation recording the paths of contemporary architecture for the time to come.

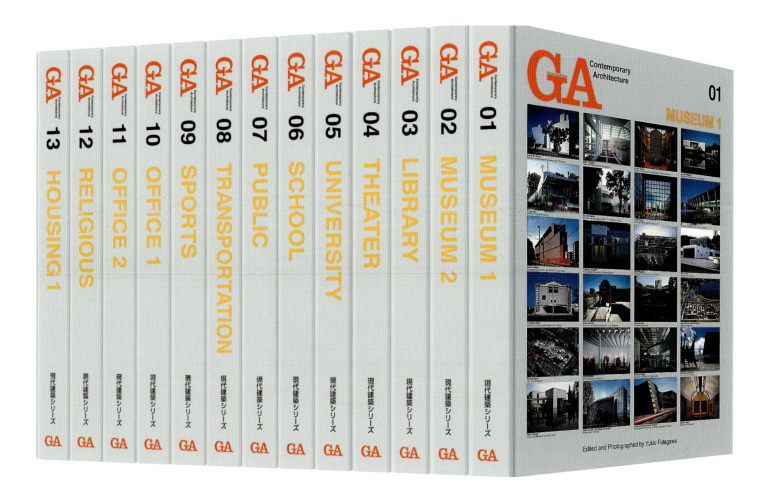

13 HOUSING 1 NEW

Le Corbusier Unité d'Habitation, Marseille; **Mies van der Rohe** 860-880 Lake Shore Drive Apartments; **Hans Scharoun** "Romeo" and "Juliet"; **Patrick Hodgkinson** Brunswick Centre; **Hardy Holzman Pfeiffer Associates** Cloisters Condominium; **James Stirling** Town Centre Housing, Runcorn; **Fernando Higueras + Antonio Miró** Edificio Princesa; **Carlo Aymonino + Aldo Rossi** Housing Complex, Gallaratese Quarter; **Ralph Erskine** Byker Redevelopment; **Kisho Kurokawa** Nakagin Capsule Tower; **Ricardo Bofill / Taller de Arquitectura** Walden 7; **Lucien Kroll** Quartier des Facultes Medicales; **Manteola, Sánchez Gomez, Santos, Solsona, Viñoly** Manantiales Housing; **Arquitectonica** The Atlantis; **Piet Blom** Arbres/Forêt d'Habitations; **Ricardo Bofill / Taller de Arquitectura** Les Espaces d'Abraxas; **Tadao Ando** Rokko Housing I, II, III; **A Design Group —D. M. Cooper, R. Clemenson, M. W. Folonis** Barrington Condominiums; **Manolo Nuñez-Yanowsky** Les Arènes de Picasso; **Henri Gaudin** Housing in Evry; **Henri E. Ciriani** Lognes; **Jean Nouvel** Nemausus I; **Renzo Piano** Rue de Meaux Housing; **Riken Yamamoto** Hodakubo Housing; **Steven Holl** Void Space/Hinged Space Housing; **Rem Koolhaas / OMA** Nexus World Housing; **Frank O. Gehry** Goldstein-Sud Housing Development; **Steven Holl** Makuhari Bay New Town; **Francis Soler** Suite Sans Fin; **Frederic Borel** Housing Building Rue Pelleport; **A. Isozaki—K. Sejima + A. Takahashi + C. Holy + E. Diller** Hightown Kitagata; **Kazuhiro Kojima + Kazuko Akamatsu / CAt** Space Block Kamishinjo; **Kengo Kuma** Shinonome Apartment Building; **Norman Foster** Albion Riverside Development; **BIG/Bjarke Ingels** VM-Houses; **Ryue Nishizawa** Moriyama House; **Morphosis** Madrid Social Housing; **Steven Holl** Linked Hybrid; **Frank O. Gehry** 8 Spruce Street (New York by Gehry); **Jean Nouvel** 40 Mercer Lodgements; **BIG/Bjarke Ingels** The Mountain; **Smith-Miller + Hawkinson** 405-427 West 53rd Street "The Dillon"; **Michael Maltzan** New Carver Apartments; **Alberto Kalach** Reforma 27; **Jean Nouvel** One Central Park; **SANAA** Shakujii Apartment; **Kazuyo Sejima** Kyoto Apartments (Nishinoyama House)

01 MUSEUM 1
50 works in total, 336 total pages

02 MUSEUM 2
43 works in total, 288 total pages

03 LIBRARY
50 works in total, 320 total pages

04 THEATER
43 works in total, 320 total pages

05 UNIVERSITY
48 works in total, 336 total pages

06 SCHOOL
46 works in total, 256 total pages

07 PUBLIC
46 works in total, 320 total pages

08 TRANSPORTATION
43 works in total, 288 total pages

09 SPORTS
50 works in total, 288 total pages

10 OFFICE 1
59 works in total, 280 total pages

11 OFFICE 2
54 works in total, 304 total pages

12 RELIGIOUS
60 works in total, 248 total pages

01 MUSEUM 1 *is reprinted*

Size: 300×228 mm, English and Japanese text
¥5,700 (Volume 1 (reprinted), 12, 13 : ¥6,500) +tax

GA DOCUMENT

GA DOCUMENT presents the finest in international design, focusing on architectures that expresses our times and striving to record the history of contemporary architecture. International scholars and critics provide insightful texts to further inform the reader of the most up-to-date ideas and events in the profession.

多様に広がり，変化を見せる世界の現代建築の動向をデザインの問題を中心に取り上げ，現代建築の完全な記録をめざしつつ，時代の流れに柔軟に対応した独自の視点から作品をセレクションし，新鮮な情報を世界に向けて発信する唯一のグローバルな建築専門誌。

English and Japanese text, Size: 300×257mm

132 Latest Issue

Special Issue: "INTERNATIONAL 2015"

特集：第23回〈現代世界の建築家〉展

Projects:
Tadao Ando | Shigeru Ban | BIG/Bjarke Ingels + Thomas Heatherwick | Coop Himmelblau | ELEMENTAL | Ensamble Studio | Norman Foster + Fernando Romero | Sou Fujimoto | Zaha Hadid | Steven Holl | Junya Ishigami | Toyo Ito | Christian Kerez | Kengo Kuma | Michel Maltzan | Morphosis | MVRDV | Jean Nouvel | OMA | Renzo Piano Building Workshop | Smiljan Radic | Fernando Romero | SANAA | selgascano | Snøhetta | SPBR Arquitetos | Studio Mumbai | UNStudio | Wang Shu

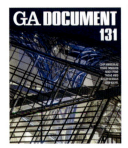

Works: Coop Himmelblau / Musée des Confluences Yoshio Taniguchi / Heisei Chishinkan Wing of the Kyoto National Museum | Renzo Piano / Harvard Art Museums Renovation and Expansion | Tadao Ando / Shanghai Poly Theater | Atelier Deshaus / Long Museum West Bund | Jean Nouvel / Château La Dominique
Projects: Jean Nouvel / National Art Museum of China

作品：コープ・ヒンメルブラウ／コンフリュアンス博物館 谷口吉生／京都国立博物館「知新館」｜レンゾ・ピアノ／ハーバード大学美術館改修・増築計画｜安藤忠雄／上海保利劇場｜大舎建築設計事務所／龍美術館西岸館｜ジャン・ヌヴェル／シャトー・ラ・ドミニク
プロジェクト：ジャン・ヌヴェル／中国国立美術館

131
140 pages, 94 in color
¥3,200

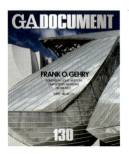

Special Feature **FRANK O. GEHRY**
Essay: My Three Latest Museums / Frank O. Gehry
Three Latest Museums: Fondation Louis Vuitton | Ohr-O'Keefe Museums | Biomuseo
New Projects: Quanzhou Museum of Contemporary Art (QMoCA) | Prospect Place at Battersea Power Station | King Street West
Exhibition: "Frank Gehry" at Centre Pompidou

エッセイ：最新の三つのミュージアムについて
最新ミュージアム3作：ルイ・ヴィトン財団｜オーア・オキーフ美術館｜生物多様性博物館
最新プロジェクト：泉州現代美術館｜バターシー発電所再開発計画｜キング・ストリート・ウェスト
展覧会：フランク・ゲーリー展、ポンピドゥ・センター

130
140 pages, 94 in color
¥3,200

Works: Jean Nouvel / One Central Park | Smiljan Radic / Serpentine Gallery Pavilion 2014 | Renzo Piano / Fondation Pathé Jérôme Seydoux Kazuyo Sejima / Yoshida Printing Inc. Tokyo HQ, Sonei-ji Cemetery Pavilion "Muyuju-rin" | Zaha Hadid / Dongdaemun Design Plaza, London Aquatics Centre, Serpentine Sackler Gallery | Coop Himmelblau / House of Music

作品：ジャン・ヌヴェル／ワン・セントラル・パーク｜スミルハン・ラディック／サーペンタイン・ギャラリー・パヴィリオン2014｜レンゾ・ピアノ／パテ・ジェローム・セドゥ財団｜妹島和世／ヨシダ印刷東京本社，總寧寺永代供養施設｜ザハ・ハディド／東大門デザイン・プラザ，ロンドン・アクアティクス・センター，サーペンタイン・サックラー・ギャラリー｜コープ・ヒンメルブラウ／音楽の家

129
144 pages, 90 in color
¥3,200

Works: Steven Holl / Seona Reid Building (Glasgow School of Art) | Morphosis / New Computing and Information Science Building—Gates Hall (Cornell University), Emerson College Los Angeles | CRAB Studio / Abedian School of Architecture (Bond University) | O'Donnell + Tuomey / Saw Swee Hock Student Centre (London Scgool of Economics) Renzo Piano / Kimbell Art Museum Expansion

作品：スティーヴン・ホール／グラスゴー芸術大学セオナ・リード・ビルディング｜モーフォシス／コーネル大学新コンピューティング／情報科学棟—ゲイツ・ホール，エマーソン・カレッジ・ロサンゼルス｜CRABスタジオ／ボンド大学アベディアン建築学棟｜オドネル+トゥミ／ロンドン経済大学ソウ・スウィ・ホック学生会館｜レンゾ・ピアノ／キンベル美術館増築棟

128
144 pages, 84 in color
¥3,200

Special Issue: "INTERNATIONAL 2014"
特集：第22回〈現代世界の建築家〉展

Projects:
Alejandro Aravena/ELEMENTAL | Shigeru Ban
BIG/Bjarke Ingels | Coop Himmelblau
Ensamble Studio | Norman Foster | Sou Fujimoto
Frank O. Gehry | Zaha Hadid | Steven Holl
Junya Ishigami | Toyo Ito | JKMM Architects
Johnston Marklee | Christian Kerez | Kengo Kuma
Morphosis | Jean Nouvel | Renzo Piano
Smiljan Radic + Gabriela Medrano + Ricardo Serpell
SANAA | Juan Doming Santosselgascano
Álvaro Siza + Juan Doming Santos | SPBR Arquitetos

127
180 pages, 96 in color
¥3,200

Works: BIG / Danish Maritime Museum | Jean Nouvel / Doha Tower | Tadao Ando / Hansol Museum Kengo Kuma / Besançon City Arts and Culture Center SANAA / Junko Fukutake Hall (Okayama Univ. J-Hall) and others
Treasure of Architecture: Eurico Prado Lopes + Luiz Telles / CCSP—Centro Cultural São Paulo

作品：BIG／デンマーク海洋博物館｜ジャン・ヌヴェル／ドーハ・タワー，ファブリカ・モリッツ・バルセロナ，安藤忠雄／ハンソル・ミュージアム｜隈研吾／ブザンソン芸術文化センター SANAA／Junko Fukutake Hall, 他
名作建築を訪ねて：エウリコ・プラド・ロペス+ルイス・テレース／サンパウロ文化センター（CCSP）

126
144 pages, 84 in color
¥3,200

表記価格に消費税は含まれておりません。